What people are saying about Ludmilla

Ludmila is a fast paced, action-packed story. Full of history from both Ukraine, Germany and Australia, it crosses many country borders and cultural boundaries. One has to ask how could anyone survive such appalling childhood of poverty and severe deprivation in work camps and yet rise above it all? Written in the first person, the reader is pulled into the story and walks in Ludmila's shoes, whether she's tramping barefoot through the snow in Europe, or watching the world go past from a boat in the Suez Canal or sweltering in Australia's basic refugee camps.

Both compelling and informative, Ludmila is an inspiring book. Marion, I salute you. This is a seamless, well written historical piece of literature. Well done.

~ Jo Wanmer

Marion Kilchester invites us on a journey through an inspirational biography of her Mother-in-Law's early childhood in pre-war Ukraine, schooling in Russia, young motherhood in a German forced-labour camp, resettlement procedures in Italy, to immigrant housing and eventual freedom in Australia.

Marion brings Ludmila and all those who surround her to life with startling clarity. She recreates scenes that highlight the highs and lows of Ludmila's life, and that of her husband and children, without forgetting those who influenced her life along the way.

Congratulations to Marion! A great read that keeps the reader entranced from beginning to end.

~ Linda Upton

Marion Kilchester's poignant homage to her late mother-in-law strikes me as being an important work.

It is written in the first person and based upon the copious notes that Marion had made and kept after long discussions with Ludmila during her later years.

The story serves as a powerful reminder that we can pass by people like Ludmila in the street, little realising the wealth of extraordinary events they have lived through.

Marion's book will help to ensure that we don't forget what Ludmila's generation went through.

Robert Brooke

Ludmila

FROM OPPRESSION TO FREEDOM

MARION KILCHESTER

Ludmila: From Oppression to Freedom

Copyright © 2024 Marion Kilchester

Published by Disruptive Publishing

www.disruptivepublishing.com.au

Cover design by Timothy Kilchester

All Rights Reserved. No part of this publication may be reproduced, distributed or transmitted in any form, or by any means, including photocopying, recording, or any other electronic methods, without the prior written permission of the author or publisher. Brief quotations that are credited to the publication and the author are permitted.

ISBN # 978-1-7636156-8-7 Paperback

ISBN # 978-1-7637283-0-1 Hard cover

ISBN # 978-1-7637283-1-8 Kindle

TO LUDMILA

and

To her children, grandchildren, and future generations

Ludmila, Mykola and baby Kola, on their wedding day, 3 weeks
after being released from forced labour-camp 1945

TABLE OF CONTENTS

INTRODUCTION 1

PART 1 UKRAINE 3

KAMIANA 5
GRAIN REQUISITIONS-1928 9
TRANSPORTATION OF PETLYURA SUPPORTERS-1929 ... 11
COLLECTIVISATION-1929 13
EVICTION-1931 17
STARVATION 23
KOMSOMOL SCHOOL-DNIPROPETROVSK-1937 25
HITLER- FRIEND OR FOE-1939 31
HITLER INVADES RUSSIA AND THE UKRAINE 1941 33
CAPTURED- MARCH 1943 35

THE TRAIN JOURNEY TO GERMAN FORCED- LABOUR
CAMP 1943 37

PART 2 GERMANY 41

FORCED LABOUR CAMP 43
AIR RAIDS 49
BIRTH OF BABY MYKOLA- JANUARY 1945 53
BOMBING OF STUTTGART 57

ARRIVAL OF AMERICANS AND SURRENDER OF
GERMANY- MAY 1945 59

ILLESHEIM 1945-1947 65

SEPTEMBER 1949 LEAVING GERMANY 73

NAPLES SEPTEMBER 1949 77

SELECTION PROCESS – MORE MEDICALS 79

BOARDING THE SHIP, FAIRSEA -LEAVING EUROPE.......... 83

THE BOAT JOURNEY TO AUSTRALIA 85

PART 3 AUSTRALIA 95

BONEGILLA... 97

A SIGN ON A WOODEN STAKE IN A SEA OF HIGH GRASS-
BONEGILLA... 101

PREGNANT AGAIN! 111

TWENTY-ONE TINY GRAVES 113

FIRST CHRISTMAS IN AUSTRALIA.. 117

A REFUGEE KID IN AN AUSSIE SCHOOL.............................. 119

WOLODIA IS BORN-1950 121

BLOCK 19.. 123

OUR TIN-SHED HOME BY THE LAKE 127

THE ITALIAN RIOTS-1952 131

BEING UKRAINIAN... 137

NEW HORIZONS-1953 139

LEAVING BONEGILLA 1953-1954... 141

PART 4 MAITLAND 149

MAITLAND 1954-SETTLING IN TO WORK, SCHOOL, AND PLAY 151
MAITLAND FLOOD 1955 161
SUSIE'S BIRTH 1958 167
NATURALISATION 169
1965 173
ABORTION 175
RETURN TO UKRAINE 177
DEATH OF FATHER 179
NEW MEMORIES 181
THE LAST TEN YEARS 183
CAR ACCIDENT, HEADACHES AND HEARTACHE 185
MENTAL HOSPITAL 187
CANCER 189

A LETTER TO LUDMILA 193

AUTHOR'S NOTES 197
BOOKS QUOTED OR CONSULTED 199
ABOUT THE AUTHOR 201
OTHER WORKS BY THE AUTHOR 203
ACKNOWLEDGEMENTS 205

INTRODUCTION

Losing her grandparents at the hands of Stalin when she was only two years old, and her father soon after, Ludmila knew loss very early in her life. It was the beginning of many hurdles which she had to overcome.

Little Ludmila had a cup-half-full personality, and as each obstacle presented itself, a strength developed in her character which enabled her to survive without bitterness. Being the only one of her family to survive the tyranny of Stalin, the day came when she was bundled into one of the notorious cattle-trains and transported from her homeland to years of forced-labour in Germany.

Follow her amazing story of survival and resilience, as she with her small family made Australia home when the war was over. Her first baby, Mykola, born while she was still a prisoner, became my husband. Ludmila became my mother-in-law, and my inspiration. As she told me snippets of her story, I wrote them down in an exercise book which I kept for years, and eventually expanded into this book.

Be inspired by the story of LUDMILA.

PART 1
UKRAINE

GRAIN REQUISITIONS- 1928

TRANSPORTATION OF PETLYURA SUPPORTERS- 1929

COLLECTIVISATION- 1929

EVICTION - 1931

STARVATION

KOMSOMOL SCHOOL-DNIPROPETROVSK-1937

HITLER: FRIEND OR FOE? – 1939

HITLER INVADES RUSSIA AND UKRAINE-1941

CAPTURED-MARCH 1943

KAMIANA

I, Ludmila, was born in a country both beautiful and austere; a land experiencing hot summers and freezing winters, a nation rich in farming and agriculture and containing huge mineral deposits, yet poor in security, stability, and safety. I was born in a land and an era of extreme contrasts.

I was born in the last month of spring, on the 21st of May 1927. It was the leanest month of the year. What grass there was, crunched underfoot, and the dams and creeks were dry. Kamiana, my birthplace is situated on the Northern Steppe, black soil country bordered by areas of woodland where deer wandered. Kamiana was only a small village surrounded by rural farmland. In May, usually the newly planted crops of grain and vegetables were thriving, the fruit trees and berries were flowering or in fruit and the streams and ponds were full of fresh, clean water. But not when I was born.

During the years 1921-1923 the country was in famine. Poor grain harvests those years meant that there was not enough seed for a complete crop to be sown. What was planted failed. 1924 again produced a poor grain harvest. Each season there was not enough grain to plant a full crop for the next season. What was planted struggled. The grains would sprout but with not enough water, the plants yellowed, wilted, and died.

As crops continually failed and the rains did not come, along with the impositions placed on us by Stalin, Mamma tried desperately to supplement our food by conserving every drop of water that she could. The used water from bathing, clothes washing and dish cleaning, Mamma bucketed and carried out to her tiny, frugal vegetable garden where she carefully poured out the sudsy water onto the limp plants and parched soil which greedily absorbed her small contributions. It was not enough, and the plants barely survived.

Mamma would take me with her to forage for wild produce. In the fall we collected berries and plums where we could, and Mamma would make compote out of them.

In the woods nearby, we collected acorns from the oak trees. The competition for these nuts was fierce. Everybody was foraging as well as the wild animals. Those we did manage to collect, Mamma roasted and ground them into a meal which was then steeped in boiling water and used as a beverage. The tilia trees, (linden trees) also found in the woods yielded flowers, leaves and bark which were also steeped in boiling water and used as a drink.

Brassicas and native kale grew wild and when fermented was used for sauerkraut. The flowering heads could be eaten raw, and the seeds were often sprouted and used as a salad vegetable. This plant was very hardy, surviving temperature as low as -23degrees.

Grass seeds, if you could find them, were used to make gruel or porridge. Native thyme grew in the spring and the green parts of the plant were edible and used as a seasoning. Rampion, known in the western world as campanula, bearing blue, bell shaped flowers was a popular find. Its flowers could be eaten raw. The spinach-like leaves and radish-like roots were boiled together with milk and served as soup. However, demand for these wild foods was great and as the drought continued, even these resources depleted until there was nothing to glean.

In 1927, Russia had been expecting 7.7 million tons of grain from the Ukraine, but only 5.4 million tons had been obtained. All the USSR was in need. Women, their breath condensing into misty

plumes around their heads, in the bitterly cold temperatures, formed pitiful, seemingly static, and endless lines as they queued for unavailable food. People jostled each other. Often shouting and fighting broke out in their desperate attempt to get food. Tempers flared, tears over-flowed and hope began to fade.

KAMIANA

I found a recent photo of Kamiana. My memory of my birthplace is very little for I was there for only a brief couple of years. In the photo, the sun was breaking through low cloud, sending pale golden and pink rays to illuminate the green, lush growth. It was taken in summer and the grass seed heads swayed in the breeze while gentle ponds reflected the scene. In the background, a Ukrainian Orthodox church with its octagonal roofed steeple, topped with a cross, shone in the soft northern sunlight.

Kamiana has two vastly different definitions:

The first meaning was poetry, symmetry, and beauty.

The second meaning, this time the German equivalent, was defined as gross, sordid, mean, and vulgar.

In reality, the landscape and history of Kamiana reflected both meanings at the time of my birth and childhood.

While life was hard, my people still farmed their own land, but the grim forces of change rumbled louder, drawing ever closer to the time when life as my people knew it would change forever.

I was named Ludmila which means- 'love for the people ', but the people exercising power over me, and my fellow countrymen and women had only hatred and contempt for us.

GRAIN REQUISITIONS-1928

Although 1917 had seen the gaining of independence for Ukraine (albeit for only two years) and the overthrowing of the Czarist regime, living conditions in the Soviet Union in 1927 (10 years later) were still lower than they had been under the Czars.

To try and rectify this problem, Stalin, the president of the United Soviet States of Russia, (USSR) began placing edicts on the country and especially Ukraine. He saw the Ukraine with its rich black soil as the breadbasket for the USSR He regarded the Ukrainian people as being a blot on the landscape, sub-humans whom he believed were best eradicated.

January 1928, Stalin ordered his government heads to mobilise brigades ready to enforce grain collection from the farms, especially from the kulaks (farm owners) of the Ukraine. Harsh punishments were imposed on those refusing to pay.

Mama recalls the day when two Russians came to our farm. Papa was in the field.

Shouting at Papa, one of them demanded, 'You give us the required amount, or you will be charged for it.'

'With interest!' the second man shouted. Papa bowed his head. He would have to yield the grain. But not all of it. The interest demanded was 500%, five times the monetary value of the grain.

If the kulak or peasant did not or could not pay, and most couldn't, their land and possessions would be confiscated, and their belongings sold by auction. They would be homeless in a destitute land.

Mama and Papa talked after I had been put to bed. It was only much later that Mama told me of their conversation.

'We must bury the grain,' whispered Papa. Then, while I slept, Mama and Papa worked as silently as they could in the dark, carting and burying their grain in a desperate bid for survival. This scenario was repeated many times over, on the neighbouring farms.

Added to this hardship, the weather of 1928 continued to work against our people. When it was time to harvest, rain set in resulting in another poor harvest. 23,000 died during this time from hunger and another 80,000 perished from associated diseases.

We were afraid of what was to come, famine, more requisitions, economic collapse, or war. My people knew that if we worked badly, we would go hungry. We also knew that if we worked well, we would be punished by the state. Neither situation would give Stalin the grain he wanted.

In 1929 Stalin came up with the answer to his dilemma – collectivisation.

Concurrently, the first arrests under Stalin of Ukrainian intellectuals, artists, technical experts, writers, and scientists were made. All were found guilty and were sent to the Gulag, (Russian forced labour-camps) or prisons. Many were executed.

The fully-fledged assault against our people had begun. I was two years old.

TRANSPORTATION OF PETLYURA SUPPORTERS-1929

My recollections of my grandparents are few and vague, things like Dido's thick wiry beard and Babushka's soft sad face.

They were supporters of Symon Petlyura, who gained independence for our country, the Ukraine in 1917. When our independence was lost in 1919 and Bolshevik rule took over, many supporters were taken and transported to Siberia and other sparsely populated areas in the sub-arctic region of Russia. By 1921 Russia had 84 forced-labour camps, known in Russia as corrective labour camps. Collectively they were called the Gulag. From 1929 until Stalin's death, there was a rapid expansion of these camps.

I was two when the Bolsheviks came for Dido and Babushka. Dido's chair, where I ran each morning to be picked up and cuddled by him was empty. Running to Mutti, she silently picked me up. I reached up and traced the tears running down her face. Looking over to my papa, he sat at the head of the table cradling his face in his hands. Babushka was not in the room either. I was too young to comprehend, but I felt it. The heaviness, the grief and the fear wrapped themselves around me and I sensed something bad had happened, though I didn't know what.

In the gulag, the prisoners worked in the gold mines and the salt mines or worked on tree-felling. They were forced to work up to fourteen hours a day in extreme sub-arctic weather. Their clothing was insufficient to keep them warm. When their shoes wore out, they had to make do.

Food was almost nil, maybe a bowl of weak fishbone soup and one slice of bread a day. Hundreds of prisoners, Dido and Babushka included, died of starvation, disease, exhaustion, hypothermia, or execution. They didn't come back.

COLLECTIVISATION-1929

Papa, tired and dusty from working on the farm, pulled off his heavy boots at the back door and with sagging shoulders and leaden steps, trudged into the kitchen.

'Oh Mutti, surely that's not borsch in the pot. I am starving.'

The fireplace warmed our whole house. A single chimney rose from the centre of our thatched roof, taking away the smoke but containing the warmth inside. We were lucky for we had a wooden floor, while many of the village homes had only earthen floors. A woven rag-rug striped in red, orange, and yellow lay on the floor and our wooden table was scrubbed clean. When not in use it was covered with a brightly embroidered tablecloth.

The small, multi-paned windows, inset with generous sills and framed with embroidered shawls, let in enough light to cheer the inside of our farmhouse, yet small enough to help retain the heat from the fire.

A large chest painted with folk-art designs and covered with cushions, provided seating as well as storage. By the fireplace stood earthenware pots and a spinning wheel. A big metal pot was suspended above the fire, with the borsch (a rich beetroot and vegetable soup) simmering gently. A wreath of wheat and dried flowers adorned a wall, and one corner of the room held an altar with its icons of Mary, Jesus, and the Cross.

A kerosene lamp was suspended above the dining table for light at night. A day bed against a wall, decorated with rugs, did double duty as a bed at night and a lounge by day. There was a wealth of colour in our home with red being the predominant colour.

Our home spoke of warmth and welcome, of happiness and health and yet in its shadows lay the struggle and strife and etched into the fabric of the house was the fear that all of this would end.

The wooden farmhouse was enclosed by a fence of woven branches, both utilitarian and decorative. Within the fence lay our vegetable garden, the hen and duck pen and our orchard. Across from the house stood our barn, another wooden, thatched building housing our hay and grain, farm tools and tractor. The barn also provided shelter for our animals, cows, horses and pigs during the freezing winter months. Firewood was stacked and covered against an end wall.

Beyond the barn, a windbreak of poplars stood like sentinels, guarding our fifty-acre farm. The farm, situated on the edge of the village, was almost self-sufficient.

The village was mainly self-governing, living our lives as we had done for hundreds of years. Similar homes to ours stood side by side, each inside their own woven-wooden fences, each with their own small vegetable plots, orchards, and gardens. At the centre of the village stood the little wooden church with its icons and its bell which tolled to call the people to worship and prayer.

We were kulaks. The definition of a kulak originally referred to land- owners and farmers. Because we owned land, we were considered wealthy. The definition of wealth was a relative thing. In a poor village it could mean the difference between owning two pigs instead of one. A farm could consist of fifty acres or just one or two acres.

The definition of kulak also became a relative term. Originally referring to the wealthy landowners, it came to mean anyone who owned land, however big or small the plot of land was.

As the oppression of Stalin widened, so too did the definition of kulak. It came to mean anyone who was disliked by the rest of the village or had made enemies amongst the rulers of the local community or village. Ultimately it came to mean anyone who was Ukrainian. Once named a kulak, you were considered a traitor, an enemy and no longer a citizen. You lost property rights, legal standing, your home, your place of work and your possessions.

When change came in 1929, it came rapidly. The changes came from every direction. Stalin was thorough. He recruited 25,000 working class, urban aktivists to help carry out the collectivisation. They were culturally, linguistically, and ethnically alien to the Ukraine. The resultant clashes resulted in anger and cruelty. It brought about radical and instant change. Loose organisation of the Ukrainian villages gave way to tight control. Just recovering from the shortages of the summer, these newcomers reminded my parents of 1919 when soldiers had come and taken our grain.

Under the guise of efficiency, collective farms, owned jointly by the commune or state were to replace all private farms. Most of these collectives would require their members to give up their private property, livestock, and farm implements.

As Stalin put his plan into action, he engaged many different groups with the responsibility for the implementation of collectivisation. These groups included local communist parties, Komsomol, (the communist youth organisation), Young Pioneers, (communist children's organisation), committees of poor peasants, Central Control Commission, Workers, and Peasants Inspectorate, Kolkhoz-Izentr (Collective Farm Centre), trade unions, secret police and other state officials including teachers.

Poor villagers were set against wealthier ones. Many families who had worked for the kulaks and hated them, couldn't wait to get rid of them.

The need for Russians to prove their loyalty to Stalin gave no incentive to be kind. Many who joined the collectivisation brigades did so out of fear. Komsomol members received direct orders to participate. They had no option but to join and obey orders.

Eventually, all these people were told to move from limiting kulaks, to the extermination of the kulaks as a class. For the kulaks, there was nowhere to hide. Some kulaks hid in the forests, but they were hunted out and dealt harshly with, even to the point of death.

EVICTION-1931

We had been hearing reports of people being removed from their homes, over the last few weeks. Our schoolteacher had been taken. What happened to him we didn't know. We just knew that he was gone, and we feared for his safety.

Then one night while in bed, I heard very loud banging on our door and then crashing as the door was forced open. I heard Mutti cry out and Papa speaking to people who were shouting at him. Pulling the covers over my head, I tried to hide, but I couldn't hide from the loud harsh voices. Almost as soon as they came, they left, taking Papa with them. I crawled out of bed and ran to Mutti, wrapping my arms around her. She was trembling as she ran to the door, calling after Papa, but she knew he was powerless against the rough, cruel handling of his captors.

Sobbing, she closed the door, picked me up and held me in her arms. As I lay cradled in my mother's arms, we both sobbed, until eventually I fell asleep, but I'm sure Mutti slept not at all.

In the morning the sun shone, and everything looked the same, but nothing was the same. Mutti knew that it would only be a short time before we were also evicted from our home. It came sooner than she thought. We could hear a horse-drawn cart rattle up the driveway to our farmhouse. Then more unknown people with their strange language burst into our house. Mutti screamed but there was no-one to rescue us as first Mutti and then I was forced onto the cart and driven away. All we could do was cling to each other and cry out as we were taken from all that we knew and loved. Occasionally, we saw friends standing in their doorway or peeping through partially drawn curtains at their windows. They could not help us, and we all knew that it was only a matter of time before they too would be taken away to a fate unknown.

As our captors drove us on, they stopped frequently at other farmhouses, loading the cart up with more women and children. The wailing and the screaming intensified until worn out, the cart's load of human freight settled into an uneasy silence, broken only by intermittent deep sobs. Eventually the cart was pulled to a halt far away from our homes and we were ordered off the cart. The horse and cart were turned around and headed back the way it had come.

It was now many hours since we had been evicted from our homes. We had been given no food or water. As we stood there together, we looked around us. We were in an empty field with no buildings, no shelter, and no food. It was autumn. The cold unforgiving winter was approaching. Already the evenings were getting cold. I wrapped my arms around Mutti's leg and cried. My tummy hurt for want of food. We were cold for we were not allowed to bring anything with us. That night we huddled together, all of us, like a litter of puppies trying to gather what little warmth we could from the closeness of our bodies.

For weeks, we trudged through the barren land, chewing on dried stubble or whatever we could find. Anja's baby, Toli, cried fretfully to begin with, pulling at her dress for a feed, but with no food or water available, Anja's breasts lost their fullness, and her milk dried up. Weak from lack of milk, little Toli's crying lessoned as he lay in his mother's arms.

Often during the night, a dew would fall, and we grabbed at the foliage, often kneeling, or laying on the ground, licking the life-giving moisture from the plants. It wasn't enough, but I guess it sustained our lives somewhat.

Another night huddled together. It was getting harder to keep warm. Temperatures were dropping quickly as winter set in.

One morning we woke to Anja's sobbing. Little Toli had died during the night. Digging a grave with our bare hands, we buried him and moved on.

Not long after, Olga, the oldest of our group, died. This time we couldn't dig a grave because the ground was hard and dry, and we were weak. We pulled at the weeds, trying to cover her but it was useless. We kept moving. Who would be next?

As the days morphed into weeks, we lost all sense of time except we knew that it was winter. Snow now covered the ground. Water was no longer a problem but what food source we had before was now buried deep under the snow.

Cupping her hands to her eyes, Marta pointed into the distance, 'Buildings!' Focusing on where she was pointing, we could see a collection of structures. Standing there, staring into the distance, then turning and looking back, we didn't know what to do.

Mutti, taking my hand began moving forward. Marta trembled, more out of fear than the cold and began to turn back. Which would win; fear of what lay ahead or the desperate need for food?

Looking back at the bedraggled group, Mutti spoke, 'We must keep together, we need to go forward.'

Marta stared at her feet, twisting her hands, 'If Stalin is in control, they will just send us away.'

'Or kill us.'

'But if we turn back, we will all die anyway.'

Tightening her grip on my hand, Mutti spoke again, 'We keep going.'

Eyes down, we all moved slowly towards the buildings. Desperation for food had won over fear, so in a terrible mix of fear of what lay ahead and a feeble hope for food and shelter, we plodded painfully towards we knew not what.

As we neared the buildings, two people from the compound strode towards us.

'What are you doing here, what do you want?' Not waiting for an answer, they prodded and pushed us into the compound.

It was a farm similar to our farm, which we had been evicted from. The farmhouse and the barn resembled ours but there the similarity ended. The welcome aroma of food simmering over the fire was absent, as were the comforting sounds of cattle lowing, dogs barking and hens clucking. There were no animals. We were in a kolkhoz; a collective farm organised by Stalin.

Makeshift shelters made of bark, branches, or whatever the builders had been able to scrounge, leaned against each other in an untidy heap. Why were they like that I wondered. Maybe their occupants were told that was the only place they could erect a shelter. Maybe the closeness to each other gave the dwellings enough strength to withstand the winter winds. Maybe it gave some element of relative warmth against the bitter cold. Perhaps it also provided a small portion of perceived safety and comfort to those living inside them.

Our captors with their strange accent left us standing near those shelters and plodded through the snow towards the farmhouse. As the sound of their footsteps receded, figures came to the entrances of the shelters. They were as emaciated as we were. One woman staggered forward. 'We don't want you here, there is no food for us let alone you. Go back to where you came from.'

It was true, there was no food, but these people spoke our language. They were our people but what had happened to them had changed them. Survival of the fittest had become the rule.

We searched for something to make a shelter but there was nothing. That night we slept on the snow, without shelter.

In the morning, a young woman approached Mutti, 'I am Elke, my sister died three days ago.' She looked down at the ground as a sob caught in her throat, 'Now there is just me. You and your little girl can sleep in my shelter, such as it is.' She drew in her breath, struggling to hold back her tears. That night, we slept with Elke. Amidst the harshness of our reality, we had found kindness. Mutti and Elke spread the contents of the rough bed of pine needles and sticks so that the three of us could fit. We slept together for warmth. Our bed was scratchy, and the sticks stuck into me, but it was better than the freezing, life-sapping snow. At least, now we had shelter from the snow and somewhat protected from the cruel north wind.

Because it was winter, there was no work and no food. Mutti and the other women would go into the fields, digging into the snow to reach the frozen ground beneath and maybe a corncob or some grains. People died daily. What Mutti found; she gave to me. It kept me alive, but she sacrificed her life for me. The day came when she didn't wake up and I was alone. It was 1933 and I was six years old.

STARVATION

Even at just six years old, I had seen many people die of starvation and I was also in its grip. We were like walking skeletons with weirdly protruding stomachs. It puzzled me that our stomachs were big when we had not eaten.

Recurrent periods of drought brought the Ukraine and indeed the Soviet Union to a period of massive food shortages.

Kulaks and peasants who were skilled in farming were forced off their land from 1929. Teams of police and party officials went through the Ukrainian farmlands, breaking into homes and taking all available food and livestock, including pets. Grain was taken. The Ukrainian peasants were forced to work on the land but were given no payment or food.

The Ukrainian people were in the process of mass extermination through starvation. This process, put in place by Stalin, culminated in 1932-33.

Called 'Holodomor', a combination of the Ukrainian words for hunger (holod) and extermination (mor), saw at least five million people die from starvation between 1931-1934 including nearly four million Ukrainians.

The starvation of a human body once it begins always follows the same course.

In the first phase the body consumes its stores of glucose. Feelings of extreme hunger set in.

During the second phase, which can last for several weeks, the body begins to consume its own fats.

Throughout the third phase the body devours its own proteins, cannibalising tissues, and muscles. The skin becomes thin, eyes distended, and legs and belly become swollen as extreme imbalances causes the body to retain water. Exhaustion sets in.

As immunity disappears, diseases such as scurvy, pneumonia, typhus and diphtheria and a wide range of infections and skin diseases take hold, hastening death.

KOMSOMOL SCHOOL-DNIPROPETROVSK-1937

I missed Mutti so much. I missed hearing her voice, I missed her closeness. I still slept in Elke's shelter, but now we slept close to each other. Elke still missed her sister, and I missed Mutti. Our tears mingled as we hugged each other, sobbing out our grief in the dark, cold, and silent emptiness of our feeble shelter. We were together in grief, hunger, and fear of our uncertain future.

Not long after Mutti's death, my life changed again. A truck pulled into our compound driven by people in Russian uniforms. Some of us withdrew into our shelters but we were ordered out and made to stand in an untidy row. The soldier walked along the line, pointing at different children who were instructed to stand in a different line. When he reached me, he pointed and ordered me to join the other children.

Elke and the others were told to go away. Crying and screaming mothers tried to reach their children. Elke stretched out her arms to me, yelling and sobbing but she was pushed back by those who came with the truck. She fell. 'Get up, Move'. The voice of her assailant was harsh and unyielding.

There were six of us children. Elke's assailant turned to us, waving his arms, and ordering us to climb up into the back of the truck. Tears streaming down our faces, we did as we were directed, and the vehicle pulled out of the compound. We bumped along rutted roads. Our journey was punctuated by detours to other compounds. More children were forced to join us, more wailing, more repeated scenes of harsh, arbitrary separation of children and mothers and siblings. Some of the children would only have been four or five years old. We drove for what seemed like hours until with its load of starving, grieving and frightened children, the truck arrived at the city of Dnipropetrovsk.

I had never been to a city. I stared out between the rails of the truck at the buildings. Some were white-washed, most were grey, but all were towering, some several stories high. The streets were cobbled, causing the truck to rattle and shake as we drove over them.

Eventually we pulled up at a white-washed, two-storey building where we were made to climb down out of the truck and file inside.

We were led into a room with long, bare, wooden tables and backless benches. Some of the little ones were crying. All of us were exhausted as we sat at the tables.

Each of us were given a bowl of watery gruel made of some grain, soaked, and then boiled in water. The gruel had lumps in it which we were later told were weevils. It didn't matter. It was food, and more than we had been able to glean for food back in the collective compound or in the forests and fields where Mutti and I had first been dumped. We ate quickly, devouring the meal as though it had been a feast. Even the little ones ate the food without complaint.

We were then taken upstairs, where they separated the boys and girls and were taken to dormitories. We were given beds with paillasses, (thin, straw or sawdust filled bags) laid on the wooden platforms. We scrambled on to them and soon fell asleep.

The next day, we were woken and washed ourselves with ice-cold water. We were told to dress in the clothes which had been piled on the floor.

All the girls had a white shirt and grey pinafores or skirts. They were not new, but it was a uniform of sorts. We had a red scarf which we put around our necks and knotted in front. We were given strips of white cloth, called onuchi, which we had to wrap around our feet and legs. The smaller of us didn't know how to cover our toes, so in the cold wintry days our toes were so very cold. Some of us had closed in shoes, others had sandals. The boys had the same as us, except they wore shorts or pants which were often very frayed and ragged. Once dressed, we were given another bowl of gruel. This became our standard fare.

The children of the Russian kommisars attended the school also. The Russian children and those of us who were Ukrainian, or Polish kept within our own tight groups. It was obvious which group we belonged to. The Russian children had proper shoes and new uniforms. They had proper white socks while we had to make do with our rags. The only things that really unified us were the white shirts and red neckerchiefs. When it was cold, the Russian children had soft and fluffy yellow jumpers to keep them warm. We did not. Oh, how I wanted one of those jumpers.

The Polish children were made to go to the front of the classroom, take off their crosses and any other jewellery or religious icons and drop them onto the pile on the floor. If they resisted, they were beaten. The Russian children and the teachers ridiculed them. If they cried, they were punished.

We were taught to read and write Russian. If we spoke our own language, we were punished. Only Russian was allowed. We were told lies about our leader, Petlyura and his followers. We were taught there was no God. If we spoke about or prayed to God, we were punished.

Punishment for these 'wrongs' were severe. Some were beaten with a birch switch in front of fellow students. Often for punishment, we would be made to sit outside in the bitter cold. We would be bribed with candies or denied food while sitting outside in the numbing cold, hugging our knees to try and ward off that cold. In the winter the temperatures would drop to -15 degrees Celsius. The north wind was bitter and sharp.

While there were many bad things about the Komsomol schools, for me it wasn't all bad. I had never been to school and now I had the chance to learn, to read and write and to learn elementary maths.

Both Russian and Ukrainian languages are Slavic in origin and both languages are written using Cyrillic script. Although the language was not the same, many of the words were the same or similar.

One good thing that Stalin did was to introduce compulsory education for children aged six to fifteen, nine years of education. I arrived at the Komsomol when I was ten and remained there until I was nearly fifteen. I did not have freedom, but I had a bed, a roof over my head, food, friends, and an education.

Often, during the night when the cadres (those in charge of us) were asleep or in their own quarters, we would huddle together in a group in our dormitory and talk softly in our own language. Because we had come from different parts of our country, we exchanged what we had seen and experienced.

'As we were taken away, we could see the flames as our captors burned our village', Boris told us, his voice choking up with the terrible memory.

Others spoke of the starvation, of bodies lying in the streets and of having to step over them.

'I came from down near the Black Sea. We would walk along the beach looking for seaweed to eat. If the Russians saw you, they would shoot and kill you.'

Janika remembered the day the communists came to her village, to her church,

'They climbed up onto the steeple and took down the bell. We watched as they pushed it to the ground. Some of us ran forward but were pushed back.'

Janika's voice broke, 'We were all wailing and crying as we said goodbye to our bell. Our bell, which had called us to prayer and worship, which rang out each Sunday, and for Christmas, Easter and for weddings lay broken on the ground. It would ring no more., It was hauled onto a cart and driven away, probably to be melted down. Our captors didn't finish with just the bell. They broke into our church and tore down the icons off the walls and the altar and trampled them, destroying them.'

'I remember when the kobzar, our traditional wandering minstrels, came to our village. They would play the bandura and other instruments and sing our songs.'

'We'd all join in, and we would dance. Everyone was happy and dancing.'

Not only were their singing, entertainment, but many of our traditional songs retold our Cossack legends. Folk music inspired an emotional attachment to our country, the Ukraine, and brought back memories of our village life.

HITLER- FRIEND OR FOE-1939

Photos of Hitler and Stalin together and toted as being friends, were posted on the walls of the Komsomol and other buildings around the city. We were told that Hitler was good. We believed that he would give us back our freedom. At the Komsomol, we were taught the Nazi salute. When Hitler first came to Russia, people lined the streets and cheered him.

'Come, Ludmila', Andri called, as I jostled my way next to him at the front of the crowd, and we waved and saluted and cheered along with everyone else. Surely, he will rescue us from all this pain and hardship which we were experiencing!

On August 23, 1939, Germany and Russia signed a non-aggression pact. In that pact, Stalin and Hitler agreed to take no military action against each other for ten years.

As time went on doubts and fears crept in. Was Hitler a friend or foe?

HITLER INVADES RUSSIA AND THE UKRAINE 1941

June 22nd- 1941, less than two years after signing the non-aggression pact with Stalin, Hitler invaded Russia.

Hitler looked on communism as his worst enemy. He had long coveted the resources of the Soviet Union, the rich forests of Siberia, the raw materials of the Urals and the grain fields of the Ukraine.

After nearly two years of conquest, Germany commanded the population and resources of fifteen European countries. He then turned his attention on Russia and the Ukraine.

German forces, comprising of five air fleets (3,200 planes), twenty armoured divisions (8,000 tanks) and one hundred and fifty divisions consisting of three million Nazi soldiers, invaded Russia.

They drove forward in three parallel columns:

In the north of Russia, they headed towards Leningrad and the Baltic States of Estonia, Latvia, and Lithuania.

In the centre, they marched towards Moscow.

In the south, they targeted Kiev and the Ukraine.

This operation became known as Operation Barbarossa.

As the Nazi forces moved through the countries, they would take prisoner, thousands of people. The Jews, the old and the infirm were taken to extermination camps like Auswitch in Germany and Krakow in Poland. Young Russian men were used as slave labour to build the massive bunkers, tunnels, and fortifications of the Germans throughout Northern Europe. and Scandinavia.

In the Komsomol at Dnipropetrovsk, daily we heard reports of the advancing armies. Russian and German aircraft fought in the skies above us. As they came closer, we could hear the gunfire and explosions.

My friend, Anna screamed, and the little ones began crying. I scooped up little Elsa with one arm, and took another young child, Jakob, by the hand as we ran downstairs to shelter, away from the screaming and thunderous explosions around us.

CAPTURED- MARCH 1943

It was in the first week of March- 1943 when the German army rolled into our city. We had heard that Kiev, the capitol of our country, Ukraine had been taken. Now it was our turn.

Some stood, frozen in fear, others were crying. We heard the door of the school smashed down and rough loud voices.

I screamed, ran to the window, pushed it open and jumped down to the street below. I winced and grabbed my ankle as I landed crookedly on the cobbles, but I couldn't stop. I needed to get away from here. I ran. But it was useless. The street was full of people trying to escape. German soldiers were everywhere, armed with their weapons. I stumbled, grazing my knees. A rifle but was jammed into my back and the soldier shouted at me to get up, kicking me for good measure. I became part of a broken mob of humanity as we were herded down the street, and another and another, the crowd of us increasing as we were shoved towards the edge of the city.

Soon, we were out of the city at a railway line where a long line of cattle-trucks was standing, the doors open, ready to receive us, a broken herd of humanity, no better than animals being led to slaughter.

LUDMILA

Pre Stalin and Hitler family gatherings in Ukraine. While the photos were in the box of family photos, today their identities are unknown.

THE TRAIN JOURNEY TO GERMAN FORCED- LABOUR CAMP 1943

The locomotive looked new and powerful. It was ready to go, with clouds of thick black smoke belching from its funnel. Attached to it was a very long line of wooden cattle trucks. Each carriage was the same. The walls were made of wooden slats, like unpainted floorboards. The roofs were metal. A small narrow window, heavily secured with a metal grill was fixed above head-height. This was the only opening for air and light to enter the tiny box-like carriages.

We didn't have much time to take in this scene and fully comprehend what it meant before the Nazi soldiers began shouting at us, 'Moov! Moov!', while pushing us forward and prodding us with their rifles. I was closest to the train and when the pushing and shouting continued, the crush of bodies gave me no choice but to clamber into the carriage nearest to me. I sank to the floor next to the opposite wall. Putting my head in my hands, my body shook with my sobbing. I felt rather than saw a man sink down beside me and embrace me in his arms. 'You're not alone, my child'. I didn't know who he was, but I accepted the comfort he gave me.

The inside of the cattle-truck was as bleak as the outside. There was no seating. Still, they kept pushing people in. A single bucket for a toilet stood in one corner. There was nothing else. As more and more people were pushed in, we had to stand to avoid being trampled. The cattle truck had enough room for maybe eight cattle or fifty men, standing. But still they pushed more in until we were crushed against each other; maybe a hundred, maybe more, maybe a hundred and fifty.

I felt bile rise in my throat, as the full realisation began to dawn on me. My body shook with the terror of what was happening.

Meanwhile my new friend, captive with me, continued to hold me.

I was helpless. I couldn't fight what was happening. The crush was so bad, the air felt thick, and I struggled to breathe. My back, against the wall was cold.

I wanted to pee, but I couldn't get to the bucket over in the corner. My bladder couldn't hold its contents and I wee-ed myself. My urine felt warm against my legs and strangely comforting against the extreme cold. The warmth was only momentary, until it too cooled and instead of warmth, it added to my coldness and discomfort. Still my friend held me. He was like a life-raft on a treacherous sea.

The door to our carriage was slammed shut and we heard the door being bolted from the outside. I heard the muffled cries of others, and the repeated clank of metal as other doors were closed and bolted.

The train shuddered, then moved. Everyone was clinging to the person next to them, even though none of us could fall because there was no room to fall. Crying and sobbing rose into a hysterical crescendo, accompanied by banging on the walls. But it was to no avail.

'Mykola, my name is Mykola', he spoke softly to me, while he still held me. 'Ludmila', I responded, 'I am Ludmila.' As the journey progressed, we began sharing our experiences of the previous tortuous years.

'Ludmila, I am married. I have a wife and three children, two daughters and a son. We were evicted from our farm. I was on the streets trying to find food to feed my family, when, like you, I was captured. I am afraid they won't survive now that I am no longer there to try and take care of them.'

I realised that this good man was here beside me, because God had provided a comforter for me. I was not alone. In this strange world we found ourselves, we were a comfort and support for each other.

The train rolled on, stopping every now and again, always outside a town or village. The stops were always brief, accompanied by clanking metal, the shouts of those in charge and the crying of the captives. The train was being filled up or emptied of its human cargo.

When the wind blew back along the train, the acrid smoke would seep into the carriages causing us to cough, irritating our already parched and sore throats. Our eyes became sore from the gritty soot. We had been given no water or food, so as the journey continued, day after day, the effects of hunger once again began to set in.

It was the first week of March when we were captured. It was only the first week of spring with the temperatures ranging between 1 degree and 8 degrees Celsius. Because Mykola and I were near the wall, we had some comforts not afforded many others. We could lean against the wall and could get a little fresh air through the vent above us and the cracks between the boards. The downside was the intense cold, especially when it rained, blocking out any warmth from the sun and intensifying the freezing draughts penetrating through the cracks. Mykola tried to shield me from the cold, wrapping his arms around me, or putting himself between the wall and me.

Peeking through the cracks, we could see tiny fleeting views of the passing countryside, the forests, the farmland, and the wilderness of the steppes. The day came, when peeking out, I saw signage. It was not Ukrainian or even Russian. We were now no longer in Ukraine, our homeland. I clung to Mykola and began sobbing, huge, deep sobs into Mykola's chest. As hard as life had been in the Ukraine, it had been my home. Now we were captives in a foreign land. Others heard me, and the realisation spread through the cabin causing another crescendo of sobbing and crying as we despaired of ever seeing our homeland again.

My legs were chafing from the urine. Most of us could not reach the bucket in the corner. Those who could, soon filled it up. With the swaying and movement of the train, it wasn't long before the bucket tipped, spilling its contents across the floor. Now we stood in the stench of human excrement. Nausea kicked in and those of us against the wall were thankful for the cracks in the wall as we filled our lungs with fresh air, albeit often smoke filled. I breathed deeply trying to take in the fresh air, but as the accompanying soot hit my airways and my throat, coughing fits would take over.

Hunger became more intense as the days rolled on, until exhaustion and nausea outweighed the hunger and thirst. My throat was dry, parched, and sore. My eyes stung, my legs chaffed, and my back ached from where I had been kicked and prodded by the gun. Our legs ached incessantly from being unable to sit or lie down for days and nights on end.

Day, night, day, night with the frequent stops seemed endless, till they seemed to merge. Sometimes cloud blocked out any light from the moon and stars. When I could look out at the night sky and see the stars, I drew comfort from them. The stars in the sky were still the same stars I had looked at back in my homeland.

Eventually, after five days and nights, the train stopped, the doors opened, and we were ordered out.

PART 2
GERMANY

FORCED-LABOUR

AIR-RAIDS

BIRTH OF BABY MYKOLA- JANUARY 1945

BOMBING OF STUTTGART

ARRIVAL OF AMERICANS AND SURRENDER OF GERMANY- MAY 1945

ILLESHEIM, UFERSHEIM, CAMP KASERNE- STUTTGART-1945-1949

SEPTEMBER 1949 LEAVING GERMANY

NAPLES- SEPTEMBER 1949

SELECTION PROCESS-MORE MEDICALS

BOARDING THE SHIP, FAIRSEA- LEAVING EUROPE

FORCED LABOUR CAMP

Like a tattoo of rifle-fire, 'Raus! Rauskriegen!', the sharp orders to get out reverberated in the cold still air.

Those closest to the door began to move out of the putrefied air within the overloaded cattle-truck which had confined us for the last five days. As we moved forward, our legs, weakened from no food or water and having stood for the entire journey, threatened to give way.

As the crowd of us thinned, bodies which had been held up by the crush, slid lifeless to the filthy floor. 'Raus! Raus! As best as my numb legs would let me, I stumbled forward, gingerly stepping over a body in front of me. A scream remained stifled in the back of my throat. As I moved out of the stench, I inhaled deeply, my lungs craving the clean, life-giving air. 'Raus! Raus!', the shouting continued as the carriages were emptied. Relief at breathing fresh air fought with fear

of the unknown. 'Raus! Raus!'.

Rifles pointed us to where we had to go. Men to the left, women, and children, to the right. Mykola quickly clasped my hand and squeezed it, then just as quickly let it go and moved away.

Bereft of the one friend I had made; tears stung my eyes. I shuffled along with the rest of the women and children along a dirt track, away from the railway-line, away from Mykola, lonely and alone amid a press of lonely people.

Digging my fingernails into the palms of my hands, I squeezed my eyes shut and wrapped my arms instinctively around my body. The women ahead of me were being forced to strip naked, leave their clothes in a heap and move under a shower.

Soon it was my turn. I was glad to be rid of the stinking clothes I had been in for the last five days amidst the stench of the excrement in the cattle truck. But not this way. The guards and a lot of others watched as I shed my clothes and stepped under the shower. The onlookers jeered and pointed and laughed. My dignity was stripped from me along with my clothes as I was subjected to this treatment. In their eyes I was nothing, so my privacy and dignity also meant nothing to these people.

First Stalin and his cohorts, and now Hitler and his army tried to destroy me. Despite all this, I was not ready to give up my dignity and belief in myself as a person who would God-willing, survive whatever was to come.

Stepping out of the shower, I saw a pile of clothes. I was ordered to take the clothes and put them on. For years I had worn the uniform of the Komsomol School, a Ukrainian girl in a Russian uniform. Now I was about to become a Ukrainian girl in a German uniform.

This new uniform was a shapeless, oversize dress. On the right side of the front of the dress, was sewn a material badge about eight centimetres square, navy with two white borders and the letters OST, also white in the centre of it. A kerchief to cover my hair and a pair of wooden clogs for my feet completed the uniform. Putting the clogs on, they felt strange and heavy. I took a couple of tentative steps. 'Raus, Raus'. There was no time to think about it. In my new uniform, I moved on.

A class system was formulated to rank fremdarbeiter, (foreign workers brought to Germany to work for the Reich).

Based on layers of increasingly less privileged and more despised workers, I was labelled OST, short for osterbeiter-forced labourers from eastern countries such as Russia and Ukraine. We were third from the bottom in the Reich class distinction.

Below us were those from Poland who wore a purple patch with a white P in its centre.

FORCED LABOUR CAMP

At the bottom of the ranking were the Jews who were sent to extermination camps where they were killed.

We were all regarded as sub-human and were particularly exposed to the whims of the Gestapo. We were beaten, raped, starved, and humiliated. Love and compassion had no place here.

After we had showered and changed into our uniform, we were lined up and had to wait in a queue where more uniformed guards were writing in a book. We were registered and given a number. From then on, we were always called by our individual numbers. They only ever addressed us by our numbers. It was just another method they used to dehumanise us.

We were led further on until we came to a cluster of identical, long narrow buildings. Built of wood, unpainted and a depressing grey, they were monotonous in their sameness. The camp was barricaded with barbed wire fencing, separated from the men's barracks, and always guarded.

Inside, the building was basic. Crude beds jutted out, like soldiers at attention, along both walls. There was nothing else. Each one of us was assigned a bed. This was the women's quarters. It was now my home, such as it was. It really wasn't all that different to the dormitory of the Komsomol, just another depravity which in truth had been my lot for the last thirteen years of my fifteen-year life.

Some of the women wept, but totally worn out by the horrific train journey and the trauma of today we all lay on our beds and were soon asleep. The fact that we even had a bed and could lie down was in a way a gift and we slept the sleep of exhaustion.

'Aufstehen! Aufstehen!'. The woman guard stomped her way along the dormitory, shouting at us to 'Get up'. If anyone took too long, she would shout and strike that person. It was still pitch-black outside and freezing, both inside and out. It was 4.00 a.m. We were given only thirty to forty-five minutes to get dressed, make our beds, and clean the barracks. The toilet and washing facilities were shared by everyone in the barracks, about two thousand of us. The water was dirty and there was no soap. There was also no toilet paper.

We were then, lined up for morning rollcall. They counted us all twice and if someone had died or was sick and didn't turn up for rollcall, they would count us again, regardless of the weather.

We had each been given a work detail on that first day. Surrounding the barracks were fields where grain and vegetables grew. After rollcall we were marched to the fields where we would dig and harvest the crops.

We were allocated a wage of sorts. It was almost nothing. The form of payment could only be used for very basic and very limited things from the camp store. It was useless anywhere else. Furthermore, whether we got paid or not depended on the mood of the guards on duty at that time.

While marching to and from the farms, the guards would make us learn songs which we had to sing. The songs would be cruel, taunting songs about us, and as we sang them, we would be jeered and laughed at. If we cried or refused to sing them, they would punish us. If anyone fell behind, she would be severely punished or tortured.

There would be a very brief reprieve for lunch at noon and then back to work. We worked in those fields in all kinds of weather, twelve hours a day, six days a week. Work would finish between 5.00 p.m. and 6.00p.m. each day, or sundown in winter. Sometimes we would be forced to work throughout the night. The next day we would be forced out of bed at 4.00 a.m. as usual and marched back to the fields for another twelve-hour-day.

My feet soon became blistered from the wooden clogs. I ached all over. My back hurt from the long hours of bending. I remember straightening up to ease the pain in my back, only to be struck by the guard. Bending over again, I continued to dig.

My hands were blistered, as were my feet, which only added to my pain. No matter – we were given no mercy, no reprieve.

After the day's work, we would be marched back to the barracks. We would be given dinner and then lined up for evening rollcall. Even the dead would be dragged out and counted.

After evening rollcall, we had 'free-time'. During this time, we could barter for additional food or repair clothing. Mostly we would just drop into bed, totally exhausted. Lights out was at 9.00 p.m.

Lunch and dinner consisted of a bowl of watery soup and one piece of bread. We existed and worked on starvation rations. Today's recommendation is 2500 calories for men and 2000 calories for women. What we were fed amounted to a calorie count, often as low as 70

AIR RAIDS

We knew well enough the piercing wail of an air-raid siren, and the low, soft drone of the approaching aircraft, building to a crescendo as they passed over, till they faded into the distance. Back in Dnipeprovosk, we fled to the basements of the buildings for shelter. Here there was no shelter for us. Why provide shelter for sub-human workhorses, which is how they regarded us. The guards would run to their shelters, but we had nowhere to go.

The first raid passed over, two days into our imprisonment. At first, some of us ran, but we soon realised how futile that was. There was nowhere to run. I, along with most of us who were in the field, flattened myself on the ground, pressing my body as close to the rows of vegetables as I could, hoping against hope that I would not be seen and praying that I would survive.

Most raids passed over during the night when we were in our barracks. We would scramble under our beds or get outside and crawl under the building. At best it was little or no protection.

Stuttgart, a major city, was less than a hundred kilometres away, as the crow flies. It was home to manufacturers of automobiles such as Daimler, Porsche and factories producing electrical appliances. At the time, we knew none of this information. All these factories were requisitioned by the government to manufacture and provide the components for the Luftwaffe, the section of the armed forces responsible for air defence.

Stuttgart was also home to several military bases and the centre of rail transportation in Southwestern Germany. All these factors made Stuttgart a high priority target. It was repeatedly attacked over a four-and-a-half-year period. It endured fifty-three air-raids, eighteen of which were large scale attacks. We were directly under their flight path.

Just one month before we were captured, Nazi forces suffered their first defeat, during the Battle of Stalingrad. A once proud and beautiful city in Russia, Stalingrad lay in ruins following bitter fighting between German forces and the Soviet Union who fought savagely for seven months, from July 1942 until February 1943. Victory for the soviet and allied forces came when the Volga River froze. The upper and middle reaches of the river began to freeze at the end of November and remained frozen for most of its length, for three months of the year. The river is over 80 feet (24 metres) deep. When frozen, the river was strong enough to carry heavy war machinery. This enabled reinforcements to cross the river, encircling the remaining Germans and defeating them. During this battle the temperature was about -20 c. The last day of the battle the temperature fell to -30c. This was a bitter blow to the Nazi regime, who, up until then, had believed themselves to be invincible. It was at this point that demoralisation began to pervade the German forces.

By 1944, the Germans were being pushed back from Italy, and allied forces were conducting bombing raids on Germany from Italy, France, and England.

We were in a forced labour camp on a farm at Markt Erlbach, in the south-west of Germany, in Bavaria, close to the French border.

At first, control of us by the guards was tight and punishment was severe. Both men and women prisoners were heavily guarded. There was no opportunity for Mykola and me to meet or talk. If we had tried to meet, then one or the other of us, and possibly both of us would have been punished so savagely that we probably would have died.

By 1944, however, the German people were in fear of the

advancing allied troops approach on their borders. This resulted in two vastly contrasting responses by the German people and very different outcomes for those of us in the camps.

AIR RAIDS

Prisoners who worked in factories in the cities and further north, were forced into what became known as the death marches. The prisoners were rounded up and marched into the centre of Germany. Thousands died in the process.

For those of us on the farms close to the borders, life became easier. Many of the guards fled. Others, including the villagers and the farmers decided to embrace the forced labourers. We were still forced to work long hours, under harsh conditions and our food rations were still very meagre. However, control was lessened a little.

After work, in our free time, Kola and I were able to meet, albeit secretly. Separately, we made our way to a copse of trees, not far from our barracks. It was late spring, the days were long, with the sun setting about 9.00p.m. The air was warm, the trees were dense with their new leaves, the grass beneath the trees was soft and lush and white daisies pushed their yellow-centred flowers up through the grass, reaching for the sun. It was our own little piece of heaven, fresh, private, newly discovered by Mykola and me.

When I first came to the camp, I was forced to undress and bare my body in front of harsh people who hated me and who jeered and laughed at me.

This time, it was, oh, so different. I was loved, I willingly undressed and soaked up Mykola's gentle caresses and loving words, until my body shook with the intimate, hungry passion coursing between the two of us.

The days continued in the same monotonous routine, but now I could dream of being with Mykola again and we met when it was safe to do so

I remember the first morning when I woke feeling as though I wanted to throw up. Soon it became the norm. Because of the intense need to hide my pregnancy, I would force my vomit down, until I was alone. I would get to the toilet or just outside of the barracks before giving in to the need to vomit. Soon, my breasts felt different, and my stomach began to swell. I was pregnant.

The guards believed that the women prisoners would deliberately get themselves pregnant so they would not have to work. They called us lazy and scheming. A train carriage was set aside as an abortion carriage. Pregnant labourers were forced to go to that carriage, where they would be held down and the pregnancy would be aborted.

No way was I going to go to that carriage. I had seen too much death. I was going to have my baby. My dress was big and baggy, and I was sure that I could hide the fact that I was pregnant, just as I had hidden my morning sickness from everyone. My food intake was low, I was very small, and I was sure that my baby, growing inside me was small also. Each day, I trudged to the farm, did my twelve hours labour, and trudged wearily back to the barracks in the evening.

Rumours were running rife; The Americans are coming; the Germans are losing; the war will soon be over.

I must protect my precious, unborn child. Time progressed, days grew into weeks and weeks into months. I began collecting material and clothing which I thought would help keep my baby warm. When no one was around I squirrelled these things away under my mattress.

BIRTH OF BABY MYKOLA- JANUARY 1945

Digging into the soil with my fork, I lifted the soil, picking up the potatoes which I had dug up and put them onto the cart. A deep, sharp intense pain gripped my body. I gasped, breathed heavily until the pain subsided. Soon another pain grabbed me and another. I stumbled to the toilet, where, squatting on the hard ground as a particularly fierce pain tore at me, I felt my baby enter this world. I picked this slippery, little treasure up, cradling him to me as I looked in awe at this tiny little human. He was a boy, my little boy. I had watched a woman giving birth, back in the Ukraine, I cleared my baby's mouth and nose, took the tube connected to my son's navel and chewed it off with my teeth before tying it off. Putting my baby down the front of my dress, I hurried to the barrack, pulled out a warm piece of material from under my mattress, swaddled him and placed him in my bed under my blanket. Kissing him, I left him there and made my way back to the potato field, praying that no-one would find my precious, tiny Mykola.

The Germans had tried to cover all bases. I had evaded the abortion carriage and given birth to my son. For those who had saved their baby from death by abortion, there was still another huge hurdle to jump. Each camp had a birthing hut. When it was time to give birth, we were forced to go to this hut. We would give birth, our babies would be taken from us, and either euthanised or thrown on a pile outside where the babies would soon die.

I had escaped the birthing hut and my baby was alive, but I was terrified. How could I keep him hidden? How could I feed him when I was in the fields for twelve or more hours each day?

'Dear God, please help me, help my baby, Please God, please.'

LUDMILA

It was the 18th of January 1945, mid-winter with snow on the ground, but my baby, Mykola, was warmly wrapped and snuggled under the bedcover in my bed.

When my fellow prisoners saw my baby a fierce determination to protect and care for my little boy was birthed in them also. In the evenings they made clothes for him and protected him and hid him during the times when I could not.

A German woman, Freida, from the village found out about my baby and began to give me extra food, even when the food was scarce for her and her family also. Although she knew that she was at huge risk of punishment, she began to help care for him. After we were marched off to the fields, she would sneak into the barracks, gather him up in her arms, and murmuring, 'Mein liebling', would take him back to her home, returning him at night, when she knew the guards were gone. We named him Mykola, but we called him Kola because he was the younger. Freida would supplement him with beetroot juice during the day and give me extra to give him during the night.

Late one evening, Mykola and another prisoner were out in the field when an air-raid took place, the planes flying low over where we were. Mykola and his friend ran towards the line of trees on the edge of the field, stumbling on the uneven ground. As he ran, Mykola looked back to his friend, urging him on, 'Shvydko, shvydko', 'Quickly, quickly', but his words were drowned out as a stray bomb came, whistling as it hurtled to the ground. With a huge effort, Mykola threw himself into the verge of the trees, hiding his face in the ground and covering his ears to protect them from the noise. The screaming of the falling bomb gave way to a tumultuous explosion as the bomb touched the ground and unleashed its deadly load.

As the noise died down and the air began to clear, Mykola tentatively made his way out of the trees, searching for his friend. 'Oleskiy, Oleskiy', he yelled. There was no reply. Soon he came upon his friend's lifeless body. Sobbing, and dry reaching, he closed Oleskiy's eyes and staggered back to camp.

BOMBING OF STUTTGART

On the night of 28/29 January 1945, wave after wave after wave of allied aircraft flew low over us. Years later we were to learn that six -hundred and two aircraft of the allied forces took part. Their target was Stuttgart, less than an hour away.

The first raid began at 20.35. The second raid, three hours later, beginning at 23.30 finished off what the first raid had begun.

Almost all the buildings were destroyed. It was a scorched earth policy. Nothing was to remain. As the buildings fell, fires broke out. The pall of smoke was huge, covering the city and drifting towards us. The next day, the smoke pall was so intense that it blackened out the sun for the entire day.

I cradled my baby close to me and ran for the trees. We could hear the horrific rumbling of the bombing and see the eerie red glow in the night sky in the far distance. As each wave of aircraft passed over and the next wave of thunderous rumbling of the bombing reached our ears, we lay, cowering on the freezing ground under leafless trees. Nobody slept that night, fearing that if we did, we would never wake again. Baby Kola was ten days old.

The skies remained quiet since that horrific night when Stuttgart had been destroyed, including the rail-links, and the food supply chain.

Freida told me of German soldiers, now broken, dispirited men, passing through the village. Like a torch beaming it's light up through floorboards and being crushed as the gap was pushed shut, destroying the torch, and extinguishing its brightness; so too were those soldiers crushed and their fervour to fight for their country became non-existent.

She continued, 'There are many soldiers, not marching as a unit, but as a remnant of stragglers, trying to find their way home'.

Raising her hands to the sky, but looking to the ground, she cried, 'Es gibt keine hoffnung, (there is no hope').

Maybe a week later, Freida took me aside, 'The Americans are at the border; long convoys of army trucks filled with American soldiers and army tanks. They are only days away, 'Vielleicht nur stunden', maybe only hours.'

Looking at Freida, for the first time as another human being, without labelling her as a German, I saw her tears and felt her fear and hurt. Wrapping my arms around her, I hugged her tight. Yes, she was German and free; I was an osterbeiter and captive. We were on opposite sides of this horrible war. I owed my baby's life to her because she reached across the divide to help when it was needed.

Holding me, she pleaded, 'Please tell them, I'm a good person, tell them I help you'.

'Ja', I replied, 'I will tell them'. She released me and hurried away.

While fear was growing in the Germans, hope was rising amongst us, the prisoners.

ARRIVAL OF AMERICANS AND SURRENDER OF GERMANY- MAY 1945

On the 5th of May, 1945, the Americans, in their army trucks, rolled into the village. The guards had already fled from here. We lined the road, cheering, crying, and hugging each other.

The Americans jumped down out of their trucks and mingled with us, giving the children sweets. They met us with smiles. Yes, glorious smiles.

Smiles had replaced scowls,

Laughter had replaced harsh orders,

Kindness had replaced cruelty,

Hope had replaced despair.

A young soldier approached me and asked to hold my baby. At first, I held my baby tighter, but when I fully realised that we were safe, I handed my precious son over to him. He gently took my son, rocking him in his arms and stroking Kola's cheeks. Tears were trickling down the soldier's face. He pulled two much-handled, dog-eared photos out of his pocket and held them out for me to see. One photo was of this soldier with his beautiful young wife; the second photo was of a baby, his son, much the same age as my little Kola.

That day, the 5th of May 1945, the German Army Group G surrendered in Bavaria.

Three days earlier, on the 2nd of May, German forces in the Netherlands, North-Western Germany and Denmark surrendered. German forces surrendered in Italy.

May 7th All German forces surrendered unconditionally at 2.41 A.M. at Reims.

May 8th - V.E. Day – Victory for Europe was proclaimed

May 13th The last German resistances ceased in Czechoslovakia, thus ending the fighting in Europe.

When the Americans arrived and we were no longer held captive, our relief was palpable. Even so, our needs were many and varied.

All of us were malnourished, a large proportion were ill, and some were dying. We had all experienced trauma and it left us distrustful, apprehensive, depressed. We were unclean because of the dirty water, and we were lice-ridden.

My immediate need was for my baby. The soldiers began handing out food, sanitary requirements such as soap and toothpaste, toilet paper and soothing, healing ointments and medications. I reached out and half fearful, half expectant, touched the soldier's arm. With much sign language, I asked, 'Please can I have milk and food for my baby?' As with the soldier who had cradled my baby, again I was rewarded with kindness, and my baby received what he needed.

Along with the American army, other groups followed quickly, joining them in helping us. The United Nations Relief and Rehabilitation Administration, (UNRRA) took responsibility for the administration of displaced persons in Europe, while military authorities provided transportation, supplies and security.

Charitable organisations provided humanitarian relief and services. One of these organisations was the Ukrainian American Relief Committee.

It wasn't long before we began organising groups and events within our camp. We set up church meetings where we were able to worship freely in our own language and belief systems.

ARRIVAL OF AMERICANS AND SURRENDER OF GERMANY- MAY 1945

Crude instruments were fashioned and once again, we sang and danced and began to resurrect our lost folklore. Many of the songs and dances were new to me, but I was eager to learn, and the older folk were just as eager to teach me. Pride in who we were and in the countries of our origin began to surface again.

Mykola held me and baby Mykola in his arms. Looking intently at me, he dropped to his knees, 'Ya tebe lyublyu!' ('Will you be my wife?')

Tears, unstoppable, flowed down my cheeks, as I stuttered my reply, 'Tak, ya budu' (Yes, I will).

Later that day, we approached the soldier in charge. 'We want to get married!' He grinned and pulled out a sheet of paper from his file, 'Look! So do these!' We were not the first! Several couples were listed on that sheet. We had only been free, one week.

'We have arranged for the Catholic priest from Wilhelmsdorf to come here on the 25th of May to perform the ceremony', he boomed, as happy as we were, about the weddings. It was now the 12th of May. That meant we had an engagement of only thirteen days before our wedding.

After leaving Mykola, I ran to Freida's house, 'Freida, I am getting married in just thirteen days,' the words tumbled out, 'and I don't have anything to wear!'

'Kommen Sie', Freida grabbed my hand and pulled me into her bedroom. Delving into a chest at the foot of her bed, she drew out a pillowcase with something in it. 'It is my wedding dress, I kept it and I am sure it will fit you,' she exclaimed, as she lovingly held the dress up to the light.

It was a beautiful, ivory coloured dress, trimmed with lace and decorated at the bodice and sleeves with bright red flowers, bottle-green leaves, and delicate lines of patterning in blue, green, and lemon.

'Oh', I raised my hands to my face, 'Oh, Freida, it is lovely!' Back home, brides used to wear white or ivory dresses, embroidered in bright colours and they wore garlands of flowers and ribbons in their hair.' I put the dress on and with a sash at my waist, it was perfect.

Thinking of all the other brides who were getting married on that same day, I knew that I would be the only one in a wedding dress. We had all been prisoners of war and endured the same things. I took off the dress, pressed it to my face and handed it back to Frieda.

'It is beautiful Frieda, but I cannot wear it. It would not be fair to the other brides.' 'But I can wear flowers in my hair!'

Early in the morning, on my wedding day, Freida and I with baby Kola went out to the woods and collected flowers; willow which we plaited, formed the wreath to which we added white Shasta-daisies, pink and white clover and yellow dandelion flowers, some ferns which we found in the shaded areas and some grasses which had begun to form seed heads. We collected more flowers for a small hand-held bouquet.

Back at Freida's, she handed me ribbons which other women in the village had lent her. My hair, thick, wavy, and shining from a lot of brushing was now hanging loose, no longer hidden beneath the kerchief which had hidden my hair all this time, while a prisoner. The garland, the ribbons and the bouquet completed my outfit.

When the time was right, in front of my prison-mates, the priest, my new-found German friends and a gathering of American soldiers, Mykola and I exchanged vows. Reaching into his pocket, he drew out a ring. It was crude, made from fence wire, but polished until it shone. He took my hand and placed it on my finger. It was, to me, the most precious thing. It was the 25[th of] May 1945. I had turned nineteen, four days ago. I was married to a loving man, I had a four-month-old son, the war was over, I was free, and I had a future to look forward to.

And then we partied. The weather was kind, we sang and danced, laughed, and ate, an international mix of at least five nationalities, united and happy.

ILLESHEIM 1945-1947

The next day, we were moved to Illesheim, twenty-two kilometres away. Six weeks earlier, in April, the Americans had taken over the airfield and barracks which had been integral for the Luftwaffe. The barracks were enclosed with high impenetrable wire fences by the Americans and became a prison for German prisoners-of-war. The airfield and hangers were then used by the allied forces. Mykola was assigned work at the airfield as an auto-mechanic, repairing and maintaining the American planes, trucks, and machinery.

While the airfield and barracks were large, the village of Illesheim was only small. The buildings were a mix of stone and timber homes with high-pitched roofs, small-paned windows, and shutters. Many homes were decorated with dark-stained timbers, like Tudor style homes. The church spire stood sentinel above the rest of the buildings.

The village was almost a monochrome picture of brown buildings with terracotta-coloured roofs, contrasted by the black-timber patterns on some homes and the dark-grey cobbled roads. There were window-boxes on some homes, but they were straggly, uncared for by their dispirited owners. Even so, it had an old-world, story-book charm about it.

While Mykola settled into work, for which he was paid a small but sufficient wage, I got to work, making our living-quarters into a home. Freida had given me some linen and cooking utensils. As time went by, I added to these, buying at the local market. This was the first time in my life that I had proper money and was free to shop. I guess I made many mistakes but was quick to learn.

I found an old, shallow box, which, when scrubbed clean and filled with a pillow and cover, made a fine crib for baby Kola. I filled our home with wildflowers, grasses, and leaves which I picked on my daily walks. Because I had a baby, I didn't go out to work, so each day, weather permitting, I would take baby Kola and explore the village and the nearby farmland on the outskirts of the village. I knew enough german to talk to and make friends with others in the village, and with the farmers. I bought old garden tools from the market, and I was able to get seeds and seedlings. Soon we had a small productive vegetable and herb garden.

When Mykola came home from work, we'd talk. 'It is strange, looking through the enclosed fencing, to the prison. Only weeks ago, we were the prisoners, and now, those who hurt us are now the prisoners and we are free.'

'Sometimes, I look into their prison yard, and I hate them, but then, I see a young broken boy and I feel sorry for him.'

'Yes', I replied. I do not hate them. I have learnt that in war, everyone becomes a victim. We must move on, Mykola. We can't hate. We need to make our world a better place. My name, Ludmila means love of the people. Mykola, that is what I must do, That, is what we both must do.' I hugged him and he hugged me back.

As summer passed and autumn arrived, I harvested our onions, plaiting them and hanging them. Likewise, I harvested the herbs, dill, coriander, mint, and parsley and hung them in bunches from the curtain rail in the kitchen. I stored potatoes, pumpkins, and beetroot. One of my German neighbours taught me how to pickle cucumbers and cabbage. I wasn't earning an income, but I knew how to work, and by storing produce for winter use, we were able to save much of what Mykola earnt.

On our days off, we took a small sled which Mykola had made, and a saw, packed something to eat and drink, and went out collecting firewood to keep us warm in the winter.

After the surrender of the Nazi regime, who were responsible for an estimated thirteen million deaths, there remained seven to eleven million displaced persons (D. Ps) in Germany, Austria, and Italy.

Initially, our people were being sent back to Ukraine, but it soon became known that on arriving back on home soil, they were either shot or sent to the gulag or salt mines in Siberia, where they eventually died. They were accused of working for the enemy thus they were regarded as traitors rather than victims of a cruel war.

Many Ukrainians in Germany, after the German surrender, either misrepresented their origins, fled, or resisted repatriation.

Finally, in October 1945, the United Nations Relief and Rehabilitation Administration (UNNR) made the decision that Ukrainians could not be repatriated. Then began the years long process of relocating the remaining millions of DPs to new homes in different countries around the world.

Although I had passed through many seasons, life had been too difficult, just trying to survive, for me to really enjoy them. Now, for the first time, I could walk under the vibrant reds, yellows and orange of the autumn leaves and fully take in their beauty.

'Look Kola, look', I would sit my baby amongst the leaves and pick up armfuls, letting them shower down on him. He would wave his arms, then pick up his own handful, throwing them into the air, laughing as he did so, and I laughed with him. Even the freedom to laugh and act as a carefree child was something new and precious for me.

Autumn gave way to winter. The trees were bare, the ground was white with snow and the roofs of the buildings wore white scarves. The eaves were hung with necklaces of sparkling icicles. The monochrome village became a winter wonderland. We were warm inside for the first time that I could remember, and I marvelled at this winter transformation. This winter was not one to be feared, endured, and survived. This winter held hope, wonder and enjoyment, all emotions which were still very new to me

We travelled back to Wilhelmsdorf, to St. Michael's Catholic Church, where little Kola, now eleven months old, was christened on the 22$^{nd\ of}$ December by the priest who had married us. On his certificate, they wrote his name as Nikolaus, but his heritage is Ukrainian, and his name is Mykola.

Winter also brought in Christmas. Christmas Eve, we went to the Catholic Church for mass. The church was festooned with pine and holly-berries. Fragrance given off by the pine branches filled the church, adding to the sensations of this special time. The stained-glass windows shone, and again, I was in awe of the beauty I was seeing. The organ played and the choir sang. It was the first time I had heard 'Stille Nacht! Heilige Nacht!' and it brought tears to my eyes. I glanced across to some American soldiers and saw that their eyes were also bright with unshed tears

After two happy years, our time at Illesheim came to an end. We packed up our belongings and moved to Ufersheim, a smaller village about ten kilometres away, on the opposite side of the airfield and prison.

Ufersheim was also a farming village, like the one we had left. Mykola was now unemployed, but we were not destitute, thanks to **UNRRA**. During the previous two years, I had managed to build up supplies of vegetables and seeds which I had harvested and stored. We grew our own vegetables and herbs. For four months we holidayed, walking miles around the countryside, picnicking, and exploring. It was the first time in many years that Mykola could relax and not live in fear or total exhaustion. We took this time as a period of much needed rest. It was a blessing to us at that time. We still did not know to what country or when, we would be moved.

Australia had initially launched an immigration programme largely for refugees of British origin. We were not included in this. Then in late 1947, Australia expanded their programme to allow us to migrate to their country.

About this time, Mykola received three month's work in the local hospital. On its heels came another nine month's unemployment. This time we found being unemployed, very hard, emotionally. I cried often and Mykola had long silent spells. It felt as though we were stagnating. Our morale began to fall.

Towards the end of 1948, Kola was again working at the Illesheim airbase, for the U.S. army. This lasted for only two months, followed by another two months working for a person in the village.

One day, when Mykola came home from work, he couldn't get inside the door fast enough, 'Ludmila, we have to move again.

Drawing in my breath, I looked at him, not really wanting an answer. I was sick of all these changes. 'No! Where to this time?'

'This is a bigger move. We are to go to Camp Kaserne, at Bad Camstatt, in the northern part of Stuttgart.'

'Stuttgart! But it was destroyed! Remember the bombing.'

'Yes, I remember, but not everything was destroyed. I am to do three months training at the American Auto-Mechanic School there.

'Tak, Dobri, (yes, good). I will begin packing.'

'Ludmila, they told me that they will teach us English as well. Maybe, soon, we will be on our way to our new home in a different country.'

'Did they say where?'

'No, not yet.'

LUDMILA

We moved to Camp Kaserne Stuttgart, in March 1949, six years from when we first arrived in Germany. Mykola did his training, and we began to learn the English language. After Mykola's training was complete, we were moved to barracks in Zuffenhausen, Stuttgart.

We were examined by doctors to see whether we were fit enough to be accepted into another country. We applied to move to Australia.

On the 2nd ^{of} August, Mykola did his medical exam and filled in his resettlement forms, with help from the Americans. On the 4th ^{of} August, two days later it was my turn and five days later, on the 9th ^{of} August, baby Kola was examined, and forms were filled out for him. While still learning English, we sat and waited.

Hugging baby Kola and pacing the floor, I turned to Mykola, 'Do you think we'll pass? 'Do you think they will accept us? Hugging us both, Mykola spoke slowly, 'We must wait and see. Three weeks later, on the 26th ^{of} August, we learnt that we were all accepted. Time to pack again.

Kola's Christening Certificate, 1945. His name is Mykola but was misnamed on the certificate as Nikolaus, a German equivalent.

Resettlement form for Ludmila, 1949, prior to leaving Germany for Naples.

SEPTEMBER 1949 LEAVING GERMANY

At Zuffernhausen, while learning English, filling in forms and getting through the medical examinations, we were also given trunks or chests to pack our belongings in. Mykola and I were given three glory-box size chests made of plywood. Little Kola, only four-years old did not have a lot, so the three boxes were ample for me to pack enough for us to begin life again in Australia. Into them, I packed my kitchen utensils, linen, and blankets, and what we had managed to accumulate over the past four years. We also had a smaller bag each, into which we packed an extra jumper and things we would need for the train journey and our documents. Because we had moved several times during the last few years, I had become adept at packing. Breakables, like crockery, I carefully wrapped in the sheets and clothing, cushioning them against rough handling.

When I left Markt Erlbach, after our wedding, Freida had hugged me, pressing a very small package into my hand, 'To remember me by, open it when you have settled into your new home.' I did as she had asked. Carefully unwrapping it, I lifted out two lengths of embroidered ribbon which I had been lent and had worn in my hair, on my wedding day. Now, I carefully placed this precious memento in the chest which had my name on it. It was my special link between Europe and Australia, between the old and the new.

While Mykola struggled with learning English, for me, languages came easily. As my English skills improved, I now had four languages I could speak: Ukrainian, (my native tongue), Russian, forced on me by the Russian occupation of my country, some German, and now English.

Within a week of being accepted by Australia, our chests were collected and taken to the railway station. We followed in army trucks, once more finding ourselves lined up, ready to board the train. While some were fearful, for most of us there was anticipation of good things to come and excitement for what lay ahead.

Mykola hoisted Kola onto his shoulders, 'Look, see the engine', pointing to the big black steam-engine. 'See the carriages lined up behind it. We will be travelling in this train, all the way to Italy, all night and most of tomorrow.'

Little Kola's eyes were bright with excitement, pointing at the engine and at the steam rising from its chimney, 'Look Papa, it is breathing! ', he exclaimed, as the engine puffed out a small cloud of steam.

I strained to see over the crowd of heads. My first and only experience held only terrifying memories. Again, I felt Mykola's arm around me, comforting and reassuring. That last train had only walls and heavy barred doors. It represented five days and nights of unrelenting hell.

'Look, Ludmila, look, the carriages have windows!'

'Yes, I can see, lots of windows!'

'And Ludmila, there are seats to sit on!'

Unlike last time when we were forced into those airless, windowless carriages, at gunpoint; this time, those shepherding us into the train, did it kindly and efficiently, seeing that we were all seated. The windows were open, and we could see out. The carriages were wooden, like the other train, but this one was welcoming and comfortable. It was the beginning of autumn, and already the nights and early mornings were cool. Looking around at everyone, we were all wearing our warm coats and scarves.

SEPTEMBER 1949 LEAVING GERMANY

Little Kola was like a jack-in-the-box. He couldn't contain his excitement as he bounced around on our knees.

The doors were shut, the engine blew its whistle, its chimneys puffed out smoke and steam and the long line of carriages shuddered and began to move. We were leaving Germany, not as prisoners but as free people.

As the train trundled through Stuttgart, we could see heaps of rubble, and bomb- damaged buildings, the result of what we had heard from a distance, while still in the forced-labour camp, when Kola was only ten days old.

This time, we were able to use a proper toilet, we had food and drink, and we were able to sleep in absolute comfort, compared to that first train journey into Germany, nearly seven years earlier. Once darkness fell, the motion of the train, along with the emotional tiredness from the weeks leading up to the trip, soon lulled us into sleep.

When we woke, we were in Italy. As in Germany, as we passed through the country, we could see that this country too was ravaged by the bombings which took place throughout Europe.

Arriving in Naples, we left the train, not really knowing what the next move would be, but we all knew this was our last stop in, and our departure point from, Europe, which was our heritage our culture and our past.

NAPLES SEPTEMBER 1949

Naples was very different to the cities of Stuttgart in Germany and Dnipropetrovsk in the Ukraine; the two cities which I remembered.

The city of Naples had rows of very tall buildings separated by narrow paved lanes.

'Mama, look', Kola pointed skywards, where, strung across the streets were many lines, each adorned with washing; sheets, towels, clothes, all hung out to dry. I stared too. I had never seen washing hung out like this before. More washing was draped over balconies. Naples had bunting, not of flags, but of washing.

To me, it was a city of arches. Some windows were set in arches. Arches stretched across lanes and streets. We craned our necks as we passed under them. Dotted throughout the city were more alcoves set into stone walls, housing statues and icons of the Virgin Mary and other saints.

Life, it seemed, took place on the paved streets. Women sat on the paving with woven baskets containing fruit, vegetables, and loaves of bread. A woman had taken a chair out into the street and was busy cutting someone's hair – an outdoor hairdresser! There were donkey-drawn wooden carts, groups of women sitting in circles on chairs or boxes, talking and getting what sunlight there was on offer.

Poorly dressed children played on the streets. In one street we saw children picking through a pile of rubble, left over from the bombing. We passed by some bombed out shells of buildings standing defiantly, reminders of a war, just past.

I saw a strange thing on one street. Pointing to it, I asked Mykola, 'What is that?' It was a set of fancy, metal cubicles, open to the street. As we looked at it, a man went into one of them, and the question was quickly answered. They were a set of urinals for men to use. They had no doors on them. I quickly covered my mouth with my hand, and turned away, stifling my giggles.

Another thing that intrigued us was a tree. Standing on a rise overlooking the city of Naples and the Neapolitan Gulf, it resembled in shape, an umbrella with its branches spreading out like spokes of an umbrella, and its leaves providing the canopy at its top. The leaves resembled pine-needles. We later learnt that this tree was known as The Pine of Naples, and indeed, it was a pine-tree but totally unlike any pine-trees we had seen before in Germany or Ukraine.

Looking into the distance, across the bay, stood twin mountain peaks. These we were told were the distinctive peaks of the volcano known as Mt. Vesuvius. A column of smoke ascended from its peak, telling us that it was still active. A person, standing next to me pointing to the volcano, told me, 'It erupted in AD79, sending lava and ash down the other side of the mountain. It destroyed and buried the two cities of Pompeii and Herculaneum.'

I had never seen a volcano before. I knew nothing about them but looking at its smoking top and knowing the destruction and loss of life it had caused gave me a sense of awe and respect for that not too far distant mountain. Shuddering, I thought, 'It had better not erupt again and come this way, not while I am here.'

I think the thing that impacted me most about that city while I stayed there was the colour, black. Most of the women were dressed in black or dark colours such as navy blue or brown. A lot of the men had died or were missing, and many women wore black as a symbol of grief and mourning.

The buildings, covered in the grey-black grime of age and of the bombing echoed the weary drabness of the women's clothing. When I was there, albeit for only two weeks, the city seemed sad and tired.

SELECTION PROCESS – MORE MEDICALS

'Medical examinations! Why?' Mykola shook his head.

'But we have already had medical examinations back in Stuttgart.' I looked at Mykola aghast.

'Yes, but I have heard they are harder to get through.' Mykola ran his hands through his hair.

Our sentiment and our fears were replicated throughout the camp. All were fearful of being left behind or of families being separated.

Australia only wanted young, fit, and healthy people and young children who would learn English, Australia's language, and who would assimilate quickly into Australian culture.

Men were forced to strip completely, women to the waist. If a man had his blood group tattooed under his arm, it was indicative that he was an ex-member of the Gestapo S.S., and he would be rejected. This total strip search also revealed if he was circumcised. This also applied to male children. Circumcision told the authorities that those people were Jewish. They were also rejected because at that time they were not welcomed to Australia. Not until 1950, were Jews again allowed into Australia.

However, the medical team were also looking for signs of tuberculosis, lung problems, heart or congenital problems or any medical condition which would exclude them.

Anatoli whispered to Mykola, 'Kyrylo has trouble breathing. He is terrified he will be rejected.'

Mykola drew in his breath, 'No, what will he do?'

'We have falsified our documents. I have had the test and passed. I am going back as Kyrylo this time.'

Anatoli had the test again as Kyrylo and they were both accepted. How they managed to do that I don't know, but they weren't the only ones to get through the medicals this way.

There were more forms to be filled in.

'We need you to sign a pledge, agreeing to work anywhere in Australia, even if it means separation from your family for two years. This is in payment for Australia accepting you into their country.' As the official handed over the form and a pen, he asked, 'Are you willing to do that?'

We didn't want any further separation, any more goodbyes, but we had no option. We had nowhere else to go. Mykola picked up the pen and signed the form, hoping that any future separation would not eventuate. We were through all the tests and had met all the requirements. We hugged each other, and I shed more tears, this time tears of relief. There was nothing now to stop us from boarding that ship to Australia.

The Americans were wonderful, gathering up the children and entertaining them. By now, the children knew what lollies looked like and more importantly, what they tasted like. A soldier would delve into his bulging pockets, pulling out handfuls of lollies and throwing them into the air. Squealing with delight, the children would run to collect them.

Kola, shy, held back until a soldier spotted him, came over and handed him a lolly, then he shouted, 'Hey Buddy, catch!', and threw lollies into the air. Forgetting his shyness, Kola raising his little arms into the air, ran to catch them.

Other times they would kick a football around, with the children chasing after them. Truly, they were like modern day pied pipers, and the children loved them.

SELECTION PROCESS – MORE MEDICALS

The American soldiers assisted us in so many ways, all the time, treating us with respect, kindness, and patience.

We continued being given English lessons. These were simple phrases and words such as 'help',

'Help'

'Hulp'

'Help'

'Halp'

'Help'

' Help'

Cheering and clapping!

We were taught to say words such as 'Thankyou', good day, goodnight, where is the toilet, please, yes, no. They were all simple words and phrases to help us cope with a different language and have simple needs met.

BOARDING THE SHIP, FAIRSEA - LEAVING EUROPE

Time passed quickly and soon it was the night before we were to board the ship. Nobody, except the young children, slept well that night. We tossed and turned, excited but fearful, happy and sad at the same time. None of us had been on a big boat before. Indeed, most of us had never seen the ocean before. So many firsts! For some of us, me included, it was exciting to be taking this huge step. For others it was overwhelming. For most, it was a huge mix of emotions, all mixed up in one bag, each emotion fighting for supremacy.

THE BOAT JOURNEY TO AUSTRALIA

'Kola, take my hand.' Firmly holding his son's hand and with his case in the other hand and me next to him, we stepped from Europe and into our journey to a faraway country. I kept close to him, sometimes holding onto his coat so that I wouldn't lose them. As we stepped onto the gangplank to board, I felt it sway, just ever so lightly, and I held onto Mykola's coat even more tightly. Kola looked around him, safe in his Papa's arms and tried to take it all in. Mykola

as usual, remained calm, steadying us, and moving us safely through yet another transition in our lives. The harbour was protected by sea walls, with an opening at one end to allow ships to enter and exit.

Once all of us had boarded, we stood on deck, looking back at Naples, as we slowly pulled out from the port and made our way out of the harbour. The twin peaks of Mt. Vesuvius, with its column of smoke faded into the distance and with it our final view of Europe. It was our last tangible link to our homeland, Ukraine. I tried to stop my tears from falling, but they had their way. Mykola wrapped his free arm around me, and I hid my face against his chest. Soon, I quietened my emotions, turned, and looked to the front of the ship as it cut its way through the waves, heading south along the coastline of Italy.

The sun shone, gentle breezes blew over us and the ocean sparkled. Beautiful grey sea creatures swam and dived, curving

in and out of the waves beside us. We later learned that they were dolphins and that they often swam alongside ships, enjoying being there, and maybe as curious about us as we were about them.

For me, as with most of us, it was the first time I had ever seen, let alone been, on the ocean.

As night fell and the moon rose, reflecting on the water we had another magical experience. We could look down and see the movement of the sea creatures. As the creatures swam in the ocean, they left behind them blue/ silver sparkling trails. The Mediterranean Sea has algae suspended in the water, which when disturbed emit this magical glow. The beginning of our sea voyage, while tinged with sadness, also gave me beautiful visual memories which I will never forget.

As we came to the southern tip of Italy, our ship, the Fairsea sailed around the bottom part of Italy and then moved in a more easterly direction. We were still in the Mediterranean Sea and both the weather and the sea, so far, had been kind to us. As we moved closer to Egypt the weather began to get warmer.

'We are turning, look', someone yelled. Rushing to the deck rails, we stared ahead, straining to see, what we knew must be the Suez Canal. Most of us had never been on a canal before, especially a canal cutting its way through the desert and sand-dunes.

As we moved closer, we found our ship in a queue of several ships, mostly cargo ships, carrying their load to other countries. We had entered Bur Said (Port Said) where we waited till it was our turn to enter the canal. Ships had to travel in convoy through the first part of the canal as it was too narrow for ships to pass. Port Said is at the northern end of the canal, in Egypt. It separates the African continent from Asia. Constructed between 1859-1869, the canal offers a more direct route between the North Atlantic and the Indian Oceans. Someone whispered to me, 'I was told it was built by slave labour.' I shuddered, remembering that not long ago, I was a slave.

'Come, let's see what is on the other side of the ship.'. Taking Kola's hand, we crossed over and Mykola hoisted Kola onto his shoulders.

'Papa, look!', Kola's eyes were wide. So were ours. Everything was so different.

'What is it, Papa?' he asked, pointing to a very tall tower with many sides. (We later learnt that it was octagonal and fifty-six metres high.) We might be his parents, but we didn't know either. It was the first time we'd ever seen one of those. A crew member, standing near us, came to our rescue.

'It is a lighthouse son, built to help guide the ships safely through the entrance of the canal.'

Looking at another impressive building, in my excitement, I forgot about manners and tugged on the poor sailor's sleeve, 'And what is that building? Is it a palace?' I'd never seen a palace either, but I'd heard of them.

Laughing, he answered my question, 'No, it's not a palace, but it is grand isn't it!'

The building was surrounded by tall and imposing pillared arches and had three large domes on its flat roof.

'So, what is it?'

'It is The Office of the Suez Canal Company.'

Beyond the buildings of the port, was the city. Again, I stared at those buildings. All the roofs were flat. Even as sweat was pouring off me, (it was 55% Celsius – extremely hot, hotter than any of us had ever experienced), all I could think of and say was, 'But what happens to the snow?'

This made the sailor's shoulders shake even more. 'Ma'am, it doesn't snow here, it hardly even rains. But it does get cold at night, you'll see.' And with that, he moved away.

Eventually it was our turn to move into the canal. The canal was 118 miles long and we were told that it would take between eleven and sixteen hours to get through it and into the Red Sea at the other end. We travelled slowly to avoid wash from the ships eroding the banks on either side. We could see the other ships, spaced out in single file, both in front of us and behind.

To our right was the African continent and Egypt. The Nile Delta stretched out over flat, green farmland. To our left, rose the rugged and arid Sinai Peninsula.

We passed through high cliff-like banks where the canal had been dug out. Other times we could see across the seemingly endless, hot dry sand, to all appearances, devoid of life, except when a small village came into view.

We saw our first camel, with its long legs and hump. We'd never seen an animal like this before. 'Horse, horse!' exclaimed little Kola.

'No, not a horse, but I don't know what it is.' Mykola replied.

Looking along the canal, ahead of us, the horizon was totally flat, with the blue of the sky separated from the land by a wide pink and orange band of haze, caused by sand particles whipped up by the strong desert winds. The straight line of the canal dissected the view down the middle for as far as we could see.

Although I knew nothing about locks at the time, I have since learnt that many canals have locks on them, where the boat enters and stays until the water level is either raised or lowered to match the level of the water in the next section of the canal. The Suez Canal has no locks because the water level in the Mediterranean Sea and the Red Sea are the same.

We have sailed slowly past the rugged mountains of the Sinai Peninsula, between high narrow cliffs and past endless desert. While a lot of the canal is a straight line, there are eight major bends in the canal and several lakes along its length. At the largest of these lakes, The Great Bitter Lake, the canal divides into two parts with the lake in the middle of these two separate canals.

When we entered the canal, the current was moving north, against us, but in the summer, the current reverses and flows south instead. South of the lakes, approaching the southern end of the canal at Port Tewfik, where the canal enters the Red Sea, the current changes with the tide.

A rail-line lay along the length of the port, where a steam train, like the one we'd travelled in from Stuttgart to Naples, stood waiting for its passengers. A prominent, sand-coloured, flat-roofed building with more arches and a tower stood sentinel over the wharf. Behind Port Tewfik, stood the city of Suez.

As we left the waters of the canal and entered the Red Sea, we could again feel the heartbeat of the sea as the ship rocked gently on the swell of the waves. Across the water from Port Tewfik, we could see mountains rising in the distance. It was a welcome change of scenery. We travelled the length of the Red Sea before leaving its calm waters, through a narrow passage into the Gulf of Aden and headed across the Indian Ocean towards Colombo, Ceylon (Sri Lanka).

'I feel sick in my tummy, Mutti', Kola, his arms wrapped around his stomach, looked miserable.

'Yes, my darling, the bigger waves are making the ship roll.' I didn't know how to help him. I was feeling a bit sick also.

We thought the Red Sea and Mediterranean Sea were big areas of water, but the Indian Ocean was far larger. As the waves got bigger and the ship rolled from side to side more, life on the ship became harder. Most of us, having never travelled on a ship, or on a sea, let alone a vast ocean, soon succumbed to seasickness.

Coming closer to land again at the Port of Colombo, the rolling stopped. 'Oh, thank goodness, hopefully our tummies can settle again for a while.' Mykola sat on the deck, wondering how long he could sit there, before having to run to the toilet. I nursed Kola on my lap and asked myself the same thing.

We docked at Port Colombo, where the Fairsea restocked with supplies of food, water, and other necessities. Wafting across the decks, came pungent aromas of curries and spices.

'Holding my stomach, I groaned, 'What is that smell?' It was overwhelming. Combined with the heat and our already queasy stomachs from the rolling of the ship, it all became too much.

The ship we were on, the Fairsea, was huge. It was a converted troop ship. It had no cabins, just vast open spaces fitted out with triple or double bunk beds.

Women and children were on the upper deck and men were sent to the lower deck. Holding Kola's hand tightly and with our bags in the other hand, as I walked into that space, I looked around quickly and chose a double bunk towards the side of the ship, near one of the portholes. I placed Kola's bag on the lower bunk and my bag on the top bunk. Kola climbed onto his bed and peered out the tiny window. I clambered up onto my bunk and tried to sit up, but I hit my head on the ceiling. It was so cramped that I couldn't sit up, just lay on my back or my side. At least I had managed to keep us together and we had a window, as tiny as it was, to look out. Without that tiny porthole, it would have been claustrophobic. I felt sorry for those in the middle of the hold with nothing but beds all around them. There were 1,896 displaced persons on board as well as crew so life on board was very cramped.

When we went for our first meal, Kola tasted it, then pushed it around his plate. 'You have to eat it son, there's nothing else.' Looking along the table, I saw that others were also struggling with their English style meals. 'Well, its food, let's eat it and be thankful.' I picked up my fork and began to eat. As the days progressed, we got used to this different food and ate up.

The communal toilets and showers were all in one long room. When Kola and I had our first shower, Kola jumped in, eyes

wide open to enjoy his shower. It was short-lived. Jumping out quickly, with his eyes shut tight, he wailed, 'My eyes, they are stinging.' As he cried, some of the shower water got into his mouth. 'Ugh! It's salty!' The showers were salt-water pumped from the ocean. We soon learnt to shower with our eyes closed.

English lessons continued onboard, but once we reached the Indian Ocean, with its large swells and vast area of water, seasickness wiped out many lessons. The complaining about the food also became non-existent, as meals remained on plates.

Passengers vomited anywhere and everywhere. The ship wreaked of White King; a bleach used to disinfect the ship. The smell of vomit and White King was overpowering.

It was worse for Mykola and the other men and boys. I was glad that Kola was still young enough to stay with me on the higher deck where we had more fresh air. Down in the lower deck where Mykola was, the heat and the stench became unbearable.

'Ludmila, I just had to get up to the top deck to get some fresh air and to cool down, but the sway of the boat is so much worse up there.'

I remember him telling me how, when a strong squall blew over, the ship pitched and rolled, and waves washed over the deck. 'I was terrified, the rain came at me sideways and fast, almost pushing me over', He sat down, 'and then when the water rushed back over the deck and over the side, I thought it would take me with it. I don't know which was worse, the heat and stench, or the wind, rain, and waves.'

So many people were sick, including the children. There were many deaths on board, especially among the children.

'Please God, keep us safe, please keep little Kola safe, don't let him die.'

Crossing the equator, it was very hot and humid. We experienced strong squalls and tropical storms when the ship pitched and rolled in the wild ocean, while lightning shredded the sky and thunder reminded me of the bombing of Stuttgart.

As we approached Australia after almost a month on the ship, the temperatures cooled, and the waves calmed. Once again, we ate, and began to be excited as we strained our eyes, searching for our first Australian port at Fremantle, Western Australia. A strong breeze was blowing from the ocean onto the West Australia coast as we arrived there.

A sailor shouted, 'The Fremantle Doctor has arrived.' We stared at him, not knowing what he was talking about. 'The wind, that's what the locals call it! Cools 'em down in the afternoons.'

Some of the ships load of people disembarked here, bound for The Northern Immigration Centre, sixty kilometres north of Perth. The rest of us stayed on board, bound for the final port of call, Melbourne.

Leaving Perth, we continued travelling south until we reached Cape Leeuwin at the southern tip of Western Australia. As we rounded the cape with its lighthouse, we experienced another phenomenon of the ocean. This was where the Indian Ocean and the Southern Ocean met. The water of the two different oceans were different colours, so that we could see a distinct meeting line between the two oceans. Rounding the Cape, we sailed in an easterly direction through the Southern Ocean, heading for Melbourne.

Once again, as in the Mediterranean, we were accompanied by ocean creatures. This time they were huge grey creatures which sometimes spouted jets of water high into the sky. Sometimes one or more of them would roll over or breach out of the water before sinking back again, showing off their big fan-shaped tails.

Laughing, Kola, while jumping up and down, pointed towards them, 'Look, it's doing tricks!' 'What are they?' he asked. Grabbing my favourite sailor who always answered my questions, I pointed towards them and echoed my son's question.

'They're whales and they are travelling to warmer water to give birth to their babies. This is their migration time.' Sometimes, again, as their distant cousins did off Italy, dolphins joined us.

The next morning, I woke early, excited, because today we would set foot in Australia, our new home. We were close to land and could see lots of trees but no houses.

Ilya, who also got up early, chewed her fingernails, 'There is nothing there. Where are they taking us?' she asked, a worried frown creasing her forehead. For me, it was beautiful. I guess I was a glass half-full person who took life and turned it into something good, something positive, wherever and whenever I could. For Ilya, a fearful person, she saw only negatives

After a while, as we drew closer to land, we could see another lighthouse, high on a cape. More people were joining us and staring at the now much closer coastline of Victoria, Australia. The sun rose over the lighthouse, turning the sky into a canvas of pink, yellow, orange, red and purple. Putting my hands to my cheeks, I drew in my breath. Like the rainbow in the sky, it was to me, a promise and I grasped it eagerly. The Cape we were rounding was called Cape Otway.

'The lighthouse is called the Beacon of Hope', someone behind me said.

Tears welled in my eyes, 'Oh Mykola, surely with a rainbow-coloured sunrise and a lighthouse called The Beacon of Hope, they are signs telling us that this land will be kind to us. I put the palms of my hands together in a gesture of prayer, 'Thank you God for bringing us safely to this place.' I will never forget this special morning, as long as I live.

Soon, the city of Melbourne and its port came into view. The ship, The Fairsea, which had been our home these past twenty-eight days slowed and birthed at Station Pier. It was the 19th of October 1949. A train was stationary on the line, and we knew this was for us. We picked up our belongings, took Kola's hand and prepared to disembark.

Fairsea on route to Australia, 1949

PART 3
AUSTRALIA

BONEGILLA

A SIGN ON A WOODEN STAKE IN A SEA OF GRASS-BONEGILLA

PREGANT AGAIN!

TWENTY-ONE TINY GRAVES

FIRST CHRISTMAS IN AUSTRALIA

A REFUGEE KID IN AN AUSSIE SCHOOL-1950

WOLODIA IS BORN-1950

BLOCK 19

OUR TIN SHED HOME BY THE LAKE

THE ITALIAN RIOTS-1952

BEING UKRAINIAN

NEW HORIZONS-1953

BONEGILLA

Stepping off the Fairsea onto Australian soil, my legs felt strange after spending so long at sea. It felt as though the ship was still swaying, but it was me, and the rest of us, who were swaying.

We were met by people who organised us into separate groups. On board, we had been given different buttons, blue for those remaining in Melbourne, yellow for those of us going to Bonegilla. Once we were separated into our respective groups, we were given food and drink. People wearing the red cross badge handed us small kits which contained things like a toothbrush, toothpaste, and other hygiene related things.

After processing, we were taken to the train, old wooden carriages pulled by a steam-train. Some of the migrants were afraid of the train, but Mykola, Kola and I were excited to get on board. This was Mykola's and my third train journey. The first one which took us from our homeland to the forced-labour camp in Germany was terrible and many people died. The second trip from Stuttgart, in Germany to Naples in Italy held only good memories for us, so we eagerly boarded this train, bound for Bonegilla. It was also our shortest journey, taking eight hours to travel two hundred miles. We travelled during the day, so we could look out the window and wonder and exclaim over this strange, new country we were in. Little Mykola had a window seat. Often all three of us were crammed at the window, trying to take in everything we saw.

Germany had high pitched roofs to shed the snow which fell in the winter; Naples was an ancient city of many arches and statues, watched over by a brooding, smoking volcano; The Suez Canal took us through arid wilderness, endless sand-dunes and flat-roofed buildings which also had many arches; Columbo's air was heavy with the aromas of spices and curries and was very hot and humid. As we travelled through Melbourne, the homes were built of red bricks and terracotta tiled, not flat, like in Egypt, nor high-pitched roofs as

they are in Europe, but somewhere in the middle.

Soon, we were travelling through open pastoral country where sheep and dairy cattle grazed. The land seemed vast and almost flat. No high mountains were evident. The sun was bright. Everything was bright. We were used to the soft European light. This light was intense. We tried to shade our eyes as we peered out at the passing landscape.

After a few hours the train ground to a halt at Benalla. This was an impressive station. The station building was a single story, long red-brick structure with the usual terracotta tiled roof. The bricks around the windows and doors were painted cream. A wide awning stretched along the length of the platform. At one end of the building, it rose four or five stories high with a tower displaying arched windows and topped with a parapet decorated with what looked like wrought-iron fencing. There were several other buildings, water tanks and multiple tracks. We were told it had facilities to service and repair the engines. It was also used to load and move local produce such as wheat and its products, cattle, sheep and wool from the large rural properties, and beer from a local brewery.

'I hear music', shouted Kola, and sure enough, as we stepped onto the platform, we could see a band, dressed in their colourful costumes, playing their instruments to welcome us. One song they played, we had learnt on the ship and soon a healthy choir with various accents were belting out, 'You'll come a waltzing Matilda with me'. The band grinned and we cheered.

'I'm going to like Australia', I whispered.

Tables were erected along the length of the platform. They were covered with white tablecloths and laden with food.

'Come, let's eat', Mykola said, and we sat and ate our fill of sandwiches, pies, cake, tea and coffee, and juice for the children.

With full tummies, first Kola and then Mykola and I drifted off into a happy afternoon nap. A couple of hours later, we were slowing down and pulling into Bonegilla.

A SIGN ON A WOODEN STAKE IN A SEA OF HIGH GRASS- BONEGILLA

We climbed down out of the train and stood in an untidy group of weary people; legs hidden in a sea of knee high, dry, yellow grass. A sign nailed to a wooden stake announced that this was Bonegilla. It seemed as though we were in the middle of nowhere. Some became tearful, 'Where have they brought us?'

One of the people who were meeting us spoke, 'Willkommen bei Bonegilla,' and proceeded to give us instructions, also spoken in German.

Trembling, I grabbed Mykola's hand, 'Have they brought us here to another forced labour camp?' Looking around me, I could see fear etched in many faces. I wanted to turn and run even though I knew it would be useless. They tried to put our fears to rest and led us along a track through long grass to the camp buildings. Picking up our hand luggage and taking Kola's hand, we meekly followed. This was not how I'd imagined it, but maybe things would improve.

We were taken to a corrugated iron building, which we were told was the reception building. We queued in front of tables until our turn came. This time we were spoken to in English. The man who spoke to us was friendly and smiled as he told us in turn where we would be sleeping, giving us a tag with our name and block number written on it. As on the ship, men and women were segregated into different buildings. We were shown where the toilets were and after our long trip, we all took advantage of using them.

I took one look at the toilet and was transported back to the forced labour camp toilet. It was a deep-pit latrine, a deep hole in the ground with a toilet seat placed above it. Little Kola shrank back, horrified. He had never seen or smelt a toilet like that before.

'What if I fall in?'

He was only a baby when we left the camp in Germany. At least there was toilet paper provided here and clean running water to wash our hands.

After another short walk, we eventually came to our sleeping quarters. Kola was tired from the long day and all these new experiences.

'Mutti, I'm hungry.' I wrapped my arm around him, 'Soon we will eat, come let's find our beds.' Inside the crude corrugated hut were two rows of beds lined up along the walls, similar to the forced labour camp. The building was unlined. It had been an army barrack, but now given to us to sleep in while we were here. The beds were metal frames with wire bases which looked like upturned gates with legs on them. Thin mattresses lay on each bed and on each mattress were five dark grey blankets, three sheets, two pillowslips, one pillow, two towels a small cake of soap, two cups and saucers, two each of soup, dinner, and small plates and two sets of cutlery.

Our guide spoke, 'There is a laundry exchange each week when the sheets and towels will be taken, and we will give you clean ones in exchange.'

I nodded, trying to take in and make sense of everything. There was an enamel pot to go under the bed so that we did not have to trek to the toilets in the dark. A small pink box with ASPRO written on it and with a letter attached was also on the bed. These along with the toiletry bag, which the Red Cross had given us when we had arrived in Melbourne, completed our sleeping, eating and toiletry requirements.

'Come, take what you need for dinner tonight', our guide pointed to the crockery and cutlery, 'and I'll take you to the dining room.' He ruffled Kola's hair, 'Are you hungry, Laddie?'

A SIGN ON A WOODEN STAKE IN A SEA OF HIGH GRASS- BONEGILLA

After a short walk, we came to the dining room. We could smell the food, even before we arrived there. Finding Mykola, we queued for the food. It was served cafeteria style. I remember we had pea soup, roast mutton with baked potatoes and steamed vegetables and hot sweet tea. 'Well, this is not a forced labour camp', Mykola breathed, and we began to relax. Sitting on backless wooden benches along bare wooden tables, we ate our first meal, just an hour after arriving here. It had been a long day and we were exhausted. Mykola went off to his hut and I took Kola's hand, and we went back to our beds. Even though we were in a tin shed, it was good to make up our beds with clean bed linen. We only needed one of the blankets each as it was still hot. Kola was asleep as soon as his head touched the pillow

I bent over and kissed him, 'We are here my darling son, we are free, and we will make a new and a good life here.' I climbed into bed and was soon asleep. It had been a big day.

The next morning, we woke early and met up with Mykola, ate a breakfast of porridge with milk, bread, butter and jam, and hot coffee for Mykola and me, and a cup of milk for Kola. When we were finished eating, we went outside the dining hall and washed our dishes in the long sinks attached to the wall.

In the sunny morning, we looked around us. There were rows of long corrugated iron barracks with corrugated iron roofs. The buildings were raised off the ground on low wooden stumps. Windows, hinged from the top were pushed part way open to allow airflow and cooling. Narrow garden beds edged with white painted stones lined the barracks. Occasionally, where people had been living for a while, the gardens had a mix of flowers and vegetables growing in them.

The large Australian trees were so different to European trees. The bark on these trees were striped orange, cream, brown and black, and in places the bark was peeling off. Their blue-green, long, pointed, leaves hung down   I pulled a leaf off a nearby tree. Without thinking, I crushed the leaf in my hands and was surprised by the strong perfume it gave off. I learnt that it was a eucalyptus tree or more commonly known as a gumtree. While standing there, enjoying the scent of the tree, we saw a pair of medium sized birds with big beaks. They were looking down at us and making very loud raucous noises.

'They are laughing at us!', joked Mykola, laughing back at them. Kola started to laugh and tried to imitate them. We had met our first kookaburras.

'Let's go and check if our three big chests have arrived.' Mykola said, and we set off towards the building we had been taken to when we had arrived at Bonegilla the day before.

Checking through his lists, the person in charge found our names. Looking up at us and smiling, he pointed back to his list, 'See, Kiltschewskij – three chests.' Our luggage had arrived. We grinned and thanked him. It was a huge relief, knowing that all our earthly possessions, contained in those three plywood chests were here at Bonegilla with us. We had a quick three-way hug and found seats in the theatre, ready for the next step of our transition into this new country.

'Welcome to Bonegilla and to Australia', the officer told us all and then got down to business. Over the next two days we went through all the steps necessary for us to remain here. We would receive payments which they called social security payments. Money would be deducted from those payments for board and lodging, with some money left over for our own use. I would also receive a small child endowment payment for Kola. To get these, Mykola and I registered for these payments, and we also registered for and received an Alien Registration Certificate which gave us permission to live in Australia.

We had two tests which we had to undergo. The first one was a language competency test. Mykola struggled with learning new languages,

'I don't know hardly any words', he fretted.

A SIGN ON A WOODEN STAKE IN A SEA OF HIGH GRASS- BONEGILLA

But it was ok. We were assigned to classes according to how much we knew. I could speak better English than Mykola, but was still a beginner, so we were assigned to a class together.

'It's alright, I will help you', I whispered. He squeezed my hand. That was one test done

The next test was an x-ray to see if we had tuberculosis, (TB). Many people had died of it in recent years and Australia was trying to eradicate it. We all had our x-rays, and again, all three of us passed. We breathed big healthy sighs of relief.

A loudspeaker boomed across the campground

'Will Mykola and Ludmila Kiltschewskij please come to the reception centre for your job interviews.'

Mykola took along his Motor Mechanic Certificate from Germany. The officer looked at it briefly and handed it back. He asked me a couple of questions, all the while writing down notes. That was it, no clues as to where we would be sent. It was over very quickly, and we left the office not knowing what decisions would be made.

For the first couple of weeks all we had to do was attend English classes, learn about the Australian currency and measurement systems, and wait for the decision about our jobs. Kola did not attend school during this time either. Time and uncertainty weighed heavily on us. We were called transients and as such, we were in a kind of no-man's land; in Australia, but without jobs and nowhere to call home. What is more, while I would probably stay here with Kola, Mykola could be sent anywhere for two years, as we had agreed to do, to be able to come to Australia. Those two weeks were very long weeks.

Bonegilla was situated on the shore of Lake Hume, and we loved walking along the shore, swimming in the warm water or just sitting by the water and trying to imagine what our lives would be like. Other times we took long walks through the campground and the bushland. We learnt to recognise the shiny black crows, the black and white magpies in the trees and the kangaroos grazing on grass a little way off.

Two weeks later the loudspeakers gave out their message,

'Mykola and Ludmila, could you come to the theatre now please.'

By now we had made new friends in the camp. Kola was playing with his friend, 'Mutti, can I stay with Andriy?' His mother looked at me and urged us to go, 'I'll look after Kola, Good luck!'

Linking hands, we made our way to the theatre. This was it. Our future lay in the hands of the Australians. Once inside, the officer looked at Mykola and asked, 'Can you make a Christmas pudding?'

Mykola's response was immediate, 'Yes, I can make a Christmas pudding.'

'Good! Would you like to be the camp chef here at Bonegilla?'

Mykola looked at him and then at me. His shoulders relaxed and he let out a long breath, before bursting into a big smile. He had been a chef back in his home country, but because the Americans had sent him to train as a mechanic back in Germany, that is what he thought he would be doing. Being a chef suited him just fine.

Looking at me the officer continued,

'Ludmila, we have given you a position in the creche, helping to care for the babies and young children.'

'Yes, Danke, I mean thank you! Yes, I would like that.'

The officer picked up another set of keys and handed them to Mykola,

'Because you have been allocated jobs here, you are now staff, and you will live together in Block 19 which is set apart for staff.'

'We won't be separated now?' queried Mykola.

A SIGN ON A WOODEN STAKE IN A SEA OF HIGH GRASS- BONEGILLA

'No, you must go and pack your belongings and move to Block 19. Leave behind the bedding, crockery etc. They will be washed and given to others. You will find new crockery, sheets etc already laid out for your family, including light grey blankets which are for staff.'

He continued, 'You will now receive wages for the work you do.' He pulled out more forms to sign. We were no longer transients, no longer in this limbo land, but employed people in Australia. Thanking the officer again, we ran back to share our good news with our friends. After being congratulated by our friends, Mykola looked sheepishly at us all,

'He asked if I could make a Christmas pudding and I said yes. But I don't even know what it is, let alone make it!'

I looked at him with my mouth open and Andriy's father doubled up in laughter. Then began questions to a lot of our friends and their friends and their friend's friends, until we finally found out what a Christmas pudding was and how to make it. Oh well, Mykola learnt how to make a Christmas pudding, his job was safe and all's well that ends well. He took a risk, but it paid off.

Because we had Kola, we were told that we would not be separated. The care of a child was regarded as a form of national service. Kola was nearly five and would soon be going to school. Adding to our security was the fact that we were both now employed at Bonegilla. Married couples with two jobs at Bonegilla were not separated. Therefore, we were safe on two fronts.

Block 19 was more comfortable. It had its own dining room where the tables were covered with white tablecloths, jugs of iced water were placed on each table and there were urns where we could make our own hot drinks. We also had a greater variety of food, such as scrambled eggs, curry and rice and different meat dishes. True to the officer's word, we now had nicer, light grey blankets instead of the drab, dark grey ones we were originally given.

We moved into our small cubicle, the three of us together once more. Mykola and some friends collected our three chests and brought them to our new living quarters. One of the chests, covered with a cloth, became a table. The other two, we stacked on top of each other and used them as storage cupboards.

'Look, the seeds I'd saved! I've found them.' I cradled my carefully labelled seeds in my hands.

'Mykola, dig the garden, we will grow vegetables, herbs and some flowers.' Mykola grabbed me around my waist and twirled me around in our very small space. Kola sat on his bed, clapping, and laughing, before he jumped down and began dancing around us.

While we were happy with our lot, there were a lot of others who were not. As I walked home from creche one day, I found Alana sitting at her door and sobbing her heart out. I sat down beside her.

'Alana, why are you crying?'

'They are sending Fedir away to work, and' with shoulders heaving, she sobbed, 'I can't go with him.'

'Oh, Alana', I wrapped my arms around her, 'When?'

'T, t, tomorrow' she managed to stutter, before wrapping herself in her grief again.

And so, it was. For many, there were still hard times ahead.

Mykola settled into his work in the kitchen, made new friends and looked smart in his white shirt, white apron, and chef's hat. I was so proud of him. He would often break into song. He was happy.

A SIGN ON A WOODEN STAKE IN A SEA OF HIGH GRASS- BONEGILLA

Meanwhile, I loved my work in creche with the babies and little children. Kola came with me. I laughed when he laughed, and I too made new friends.

PREGNANT AGAIN!

One night after Kola had fallen asleep, I lay next to Mykola, kissed him, and tentatively broke my hidden news to him. Taking his hand in mine, I softly whispered, 'I am pregnant again. We are having another baby!' He wrapped his arms around me, kissing and hugging me.

This time, my pregnancy was so different. I didn't need to hide it; I didn't have to live in fear. Good food, doctors, the hospital to care for us and shops to buy what we needed were all available to us. Australia wanted us to have babies. Australia's policy was 'populate or perish'. This baby was welcomed by everyone.

Instead of the shapeless prison uniform, I wore pretty, colourful dresses which I chose and paid for from my own money which I had received for looking after babies and young children. There were no twelve-hour days, digging potatoes, no prison guards standing over me and whipping me. Instead, I had loving people caring for me and my baby, lots of friends, laughter, and chatter.

Even as the sun shone down over us, with a safe place to live, an income to buy what we needed, and a new baby on the way, a very dark cloud was hovering over us, especially those of us who had young children and babies.

TWENTY-ONE TINY GRAVES

In September 1949, a month before we arrived, babies and young children who had recently arrived in migrant camps, began dying. Nineteen infants had died across the Australian migrant centres. Thirteen of those children who had passed away, died at Bonegilla. We arrived in mid-October. Kola was four years old and now I was pregnant with our second child.

At Albury cemetery, just a few miles away, the number of tiny, raised mounds of earth, each holding a young baby or child from Bonegilla, grew until there were twenty-one tiny graves.

Standing by the grave of a very small baby as he was lowered into the earth, our newfound peace and joy gave way once again to grief and fear. I remember the horrible dysentery and the deaths of young children on the boat journey out here to Australia. Once we reached land, we thought that was the end of it. How wrong we were.

Immigration authorities put very young babies and children on boiled water only diets for up to seven weeks. They didn't know any other way to deal with it, back then. Their little bodies, already weakened by the gastroenteritis, faded away until they died.

We grieved with the families who had lost children, we pined for the missing infants, and we held our own children tightly, in a very real and present fear of losing them also.

As a result of this tragedy, several changes resulted at Bonegilla. The authorities at the camp divided one of the huts, Block 13, into family units. Bassinets were provided for babies; extra milk and eggs were given to these families; they were given access to hot water and a fridge; the rooms were heated in the winter and fans were installed to cool the rooms during the heat of summer.

A creche and kindergarten was opened, equipped with children's furniture and toys. It was here that I had my first paid work. We had fifteen to twenty children. Paul, one of the men who had come out from the Ukraine, painted murals on the walls. I remember one illustration he did of a hen, a pig, a calf, and a pony peeping over a fence. We had an outdoor 'Movie' house, with a makeshift roof featuring Mickey Mouse on the roof. It was an exciting adventure for the children, within the grounds of Bonegilla.

A playground was also erected, with swings and slippery dip, so that children could have outdoor playtime. Little girls pushed their baby dolls around the playground in wicker, child-sized prams while the boys kicked balls around.

When we were able, Mykola and I arranged for our day off to coincide, so that we could take the bus into Albury/Wodonga for the day. The twin towns were separated by the Murray River, which formed the boundary between New South Wales and Victoria. They were only seven and a half miles from Bonegilla. Albury had an excellent shopping centre. As we wandered through the shops, we bought clothes for all of us and began to put together items for our baby, soon to be with us.

At one table, I picked up a pretty set of curtains, and held them up,

'What do you think? They would make our place look happy don't you think?'

Mykola nodded and soon we went home with our lovely curtains, as well as mats for beside our beds and under the table.

Mykola picked up two umbrellas,

'I think we could use these as well.' And so, we made our small cubicle our home. Over time, we added an electric jug, heater, and a fan.

Albury had a beautiful park with tall, shade trees, lawns, and ponds. We would buy some bread and fruit and enjoy this beautiful park. We all loved our outings to Albury/Wodonga, especially on those very hot summer days.

FIRST CHRISTMAS IN AUSTRALIA

Our first Christmas in Australia came around very quickly. Christmas in Germany was so different. I was sitting on my bed reminiscing,

'Remember our last Christmas in Germany, when we went to the Christmas service in the church at Wilhelmsdorf.'

'Yes, it was snowing and so cold, but the church was beautiful with its pine branches filling the church with its perfume.'

'Mutti, can we have a Christmas tree?'

Mykola scratched his head, thinking, 'Yes, I know where we can get a tree!'

"And Papa, can we make decorations, just like they have in the dining room?'

Next trip to town, we bought red and green crepe paper and a couple of rolls of ticket tape. We gathered gumnuts from the trees and painted them. Mykola got a bucket, filled it with soil from down near the lake and 'planted' the tree, a good-sized branch which we set about decorating.

Remembering the wreath Freida and I made for my wedding, I took a small branch of pine and shaped it into a wreath.

'Come, Kola, let's find some grass seed-heads and some gumnuts.' Soon we had a festive wreath on the door. It was a very different Christmas to the last Christmas in Europe, but this our first Christmas in Australia would be special also. Taking pride of place on the wall behind our table were the red ribbons which I had worn on my wedding day and which Freida had given me when we left Markt Elbach. We drifted off to sleep, breathing in the scent of pine and dreamed mixed up dreams featuring both Europe and Australia, of kangaroos hopping alongside reindeer, and a possum and squirrel sharing a branch together in a gumtree, while a kookaburra laughed at the quirkiness of it all.

A REFUGEE KID IN AN AUSSIE SCHOOL

Christmas over for 1949, we sweated through the rest of the summer. Everything seemed upside down and back the front here in Australia. The school children had six weeks to fill in before going back to school. End of January, it was time for Kola to begin school.

'Mutti, I don't want to go to school.' Kola shrunk back onto his bed, his little brow furrowing as tears began to show in his eyes.

'It's alright son, look you have brand new clothes to wear and look at your shiny new shoes!' his dad tried to cheer him up.

'And don't you like your schoolbag?' I added.

He looked at his school satchel, stroking its soft brown leather. 'I do like my bag. I just don't want to go to school', he whispered through trembling lips. I took his hand and together we walked to where he, along with the other children, were to board the bus which would take them to school.

When we first arrived at Bonegilla there was no school on the grounds. The closest school, Mitta Junction school, was forty-nine miles away and took about an hour each way. For a shy, little, five-year-old-boy, that added two hours to his day, making it a scary and exhausting proposition. Go to school he must, endure he must. I got him onto the bus, smiling at him with as big a smile as I could muster. Once the bus pulled away, I returned to our room, and shoulders heaving, I allowed myself to shed my own tears. I could not allow myself the luxury of being a mess for very long. I went to the bathroom, splashed my face with cold water, took a deep breath, and went to work at the creche.

Language was a problem; being 'one of them', the ones who had nothing, and spoke funny, set the migrant children apart from the Australian children. I know that he endured, rather than enjoyed his time at school, while at Bonegilla.

In 1952, Bonegilla State School opened at the migrant camp, but I was determined that Kola continue at Mitta Junction.

'He'll learn English faster and better if he stays with the Australian school.' I insisted. He fought against me, but ultimately, he had to do as I said. It was hard on all of us.

Summer, with great reluctance, gave way to autumn. The gumtrees at Bonegilla remained the same. They did not change colour. On our trip into Albury, we went to the park as we always did. The deciduous trees planted there, greeted us in tones of red, orange, and yellow.

'Oh, Mykola, there is an autumn,' I breathed, as I looked up into those trees. They reminded me of autumn back in Europe. I picked up some of the fallen leaves, stroking them, and burying my face in their autumnal colours. For that brief interval of time, I allowed myself to look back to the past, to Europe, to Illesheim, Germany and further back, to my homeland, Ukraine. Then, I felt my baby move inside of me, and my thoughts once more turned to the future.

Winter came, the nearby mountains wore capes of snow and often were shrouded in heavy cloud. The temperatures dropped and inside our huts were very cold. I had bought a small heater, last time we were in Albury. I got it out of storage and plugged it in, and soon our small area became warm. Kola went to school, cloaked in gloves, scarf and warm winter uniform. Shorts gave way to long pants and thick socks. Mykola worked in the kitchen most days and I continued to work at the creche.

WOLODIA IS BORN-1950

Clutching my stomach, I groaned as pain tore at me. Immediately, Mykola sat up, looked at me and sprang into action. He summoned the head person of the camp, who brought his car around to us. Kola was bedded down next door, and we made our journey into Albury hospital. There, my every need was taken care of by competent, cheerful nurses, doctor, and hospital staff. Little Wolodia was born on the 30-07-1950, wanted, cared for, safe, and loved by everyone, so different to when Kola was born and just as special. We were a family of four. Wolodia had good strong lungs and a lusty cry. I put him to my breast and fed him, not having to fear for his safety. This baby, I could, and did, show off to the world.

The next big event for our family was Wolodia's christening.

Ilena knocked on our door, 'Ludmila, I have this shawl from when we christened Alana last year. Would you like to use it for Wolodia?'

It was a beautiful, white crocheted shawl. I took it, feeling its softness, 'Oh, it's lovely, Yes, Thank you.'

We had also been given a beautiful, warm knitted jumper, bonnet, and bootees for our baby boy. We had another trip into Albury where we bought a winter coat and pants along with a shirt and tie each for Mykola and Kola. For myself, I bought a soft, long-sleeved, white blouse, with pin-tucked white bodice, collar and cuffs and a soft bow at its neckline. I added a navy, gored skirt, navy stockings, and navy shoes which also sported a bow on each shoe.

The day of the christening arrived, and I peeped out our window, 'Mykola, the sun is shining, and the sky is blue!' We quickly dressed, all of us looking very smart, and went out to christen Wolodia. The priest performed the ceremony, then we and our friends went out into the sunshine for family photos. How proud I was of our little family.

After the health scare, the previous year and early this year, bassinets and prams had been provided for babies. Six months on from then, a lovely bassinet and pram along with the bedding had been handed on to us. Baby Wolodia slept soundly in his snug, comfy pram while the rest of us sat outside in the warmth of the sunlight on this cold, July morning, celebrating with food and drink, lots of laughter and bucket loads of love.

Both my sons were born in the winter. Kola was born on a cold January day in the forced labour camp in Germany. Wolodia was born on a cold July evening in a migrant camp in Australia. The first baby was born in an atmosphere of fear and hate. The second baby was born in an environment, filled with hope and love.

Kola made friends, both at school and in the camp. Many happy hours were spent in the playground, kicking balls, and splashing and learning to swim in the lake. Wolodia had lots of willing 'aunts' and 'uncles' to entertain him. Mykola and I settled happily into the social life of Bonegilla.

BLOCK 19

Block 19, which housed staff families, had a tennis court, two billiard tables, quoits and darts and a dartboard.

'Come on, Anatoli, I'll beat you at a game of darts!', challenged Mykola. The competition was fierce between the brothers. Sometimes the men formed impromptu teams for a game of football, out in the paddock.

While alcohol was not allowed in the camp, an exception was made in the service club at Block 19. In the clubhouse, a bar was set up at one end. On warm evenings we could get our drinks and sit outside in the adjacent beer garden. Singing would often break out, along with lots of laughter.

I loved to look up at the stars. The night sky here in Australia was different to the evening sky in the northern hemisphere, but I learnt to love this sky too, with its different stars and constellations. Australian workers would sometimes join us.

Tom, one of the language teachers pointed to the sky,

'See those two stars in the south' and he'd point until we found them.

'Yes, I see them.'

They're pointing to the 'Southern Cross', and again, he'd outline the shape and kept indicating, until we found them. Later, we saw the 'Saucepan'.

'The middle star in the handle is 'Orion.'

We'd peer into the night sky, till we could find it, and so it went until the southern night sky became familiar to us.

Dances and fancy-dress parties would be organised. We made our own costumes with anything we could find which would work. One party was a barnyard party.

Mykola took his garden fork and old hat and plenty of straw to fill his sleeves and pantlegs, 'Do I make a good scarecrow?' he asked, walking stiff legged around our room.

'I want to be a pig!' piped up Kola.

'And I will be a big black crow, and I will steal your straw with my sharp black beak to build my nest, I cawed as I chased him around the table. He turned and chased me, until I let out a different cry when he caught and tickled me, and we all fell in a laughing heap on the floor.

Another day, Mykola and the kitchen staff gave an impromptu concert on upturned pots and pans with ladles and rolling pins doubling as drumsticks. We joined in, singing, and clapping, and stamping our feet in time with the beat.

One day, a visitor came with an eagle sitting on his arm. 'Can I hold him?' I asked, and soon I was holding this eagle on my outstretched arm. I had my long-sleeved blazer on to protect myself.

Bonegilla had a resident photographer. He was with us when I held that eagle.

'Smile, Ludmila', he instructed, as I held out my arm. He got the photo, and then again when the eagle stretched out its wings, about to take flight, while I stretched my neck in the opposite direction. I let out a little scream as the eagle took off and landed on its owner's arm, looking for the piece of meat which was its reward.

Mykola, watching me, held his ribs, doubling over with laughter, 'My, Ludmila, that was a sight to see.'

Not to worry. I had held an eagle!

A pig-on-the-spit was the focal point of another Block 19 outing. Two of the men carried the pig, already impaled on the stake, down to the shore of the lake where the fire had already been prepared. We added potatoes, onions, corn, and pumpkin into the hot coals and then sat back and waited for dinner to cook. Every now and again, Mykola and another man would rotate the pig, allowing it to cook evenly. Photos were taken to add to our growing collection of memories.

Often, during the long hot summer days, we would gather down by the lake to swim and sunbathe. We girls had such pretty swimsuits; florals, plain, even two-pieces. We took hold of the current fashions eagerly, after having been starved of colour, variety individuality and pretty things for years.

OUR TIN-SHED HOME BY THE LAKE

We had lived at Bonegilla about eighteen months. I had wandered all over the grounds many times. Down near the lake on the edge of the campground, I had noticed a small, corrugated iron shed. Peeping through the window, I saw that it contained a pile of folded rough brown, hessian bags which had once contained produce and were now lying idle in that shed. There were a few other things in there but not a lot.

'Mykola, do you think they will let us have that shed if I clean it out?'

'I don't know, Ludmila, but it won't hurt to ask.'

I took myself up to the office and made my request. 'It has a wooden floor, windows and power', I added. 'Can I make it into our home please?' I didn't think they would say yes, but I had put in my request.

After a couple of days, I got my answer, 'Yes, Ludmila, you can move your family into there.'

'Yes! Thank you!'

He handed me the key and that day; I began cleaning it out. I dragged everything outside and removed what I couldn't use. I draped the pile of bags over the fence and bashed them with my broom. Dust blew everywhere, but I got the bags clean and restacked them. Mykola got a couple of friends to shift all our belongings down to the shed. I laid the hessian bags under our mattresses. Then, our beds would be softer, and warmer in the winter. While the shed was still small, it was a bigger space than the cubicle we had vacated.

'Ludmila, this is excellent! Now we can't hear others conversations and they can't hear ours. We really have privacy now.' Mykola hugged me.

'Mutti, Papa, we can look out our window and see the lake.'

'Yes, and we can grow lots of vegetables, especially cucumbers', I added.

In no time, I had transformed that store shed into a home, with covers on the beds, rugs on the floor and curtains on the windows. When the wind blew and created waves on the lake, we could hear the repetitive wash of the waves on the shore. We loved that sound. We also loved the breezes blowing off the water into our little home, cooling it on hot summer days.

But I had an even bigger plan! I had been collecting all the empty vegemite, peanut butter and jam bottles and their lids. With Mykola working in the kitchen, it was easy to get them. I stored them away in boxes.

Mykola got out his garden tools and began preparing the soil. Soon, we had a lot of vegetables growing, especially cucumbers, onion, and dill.

On one of our trips into Albury, we bought a primus stove. I unpacked my metal cooking pot out of our trunk. I had kept it and brought it with me from Germany.

When the cucumbers were ready to harvest, we prepared the spiced vinegar in my german pot, prepared the cucumbers, and bottled them in the boiling, aromatic liquid, before tightening the lids to preserve them.

The smell of the boiling vinegar and spices was quite strong.

'Just as well we are down here, away from everyone else.' Mykola joked.

I laughed, 'That was part of the plan.'

We sold our bottles of pickled cucumbers. They were so popular, and the cucumbers grew so prolifically, that we had to go and buy, beg, and borrow more bottles. The money from our little venture was added to our growing amount in the bank. We were saving for a deposit on a house when the time was right.

Once we were in our separate little 'cottage', albeit a tin one, Mykola decided at Easter to colour some boiled eggs, just like he used to do in Ukraine. He got out our german cooking pot, put in red onion skins, vinegar, and salt, brought it to the boil and added the eggs. He made four and then repeated the process, using brown onion skins. The eggs cooked beautifully with mottled red and brown shells. When the boys woke, they each had these pretty eggs. Kola stroked the eggs; Wolodia wanted to bang them, but we managed to show him his Papa's handiwork, before we shelled them, and we ate the boiled eggs for breakfast. We had photos taken of our little family in front of our little tin cottage, with the lake in the background.

Another popular photo which a lot of us migrants had taken, was of us, dressed in our best clothes, posing in front of a car. It wasn't our car. It was usually the photographer's car or some other visitor's car. We would get a copy of the photo, sit it on a shelf, and dream, 'One day we will own our own car, one day we will live in our own house.'

Bonegilla allowed us to dream. Bonegilla enabled us to put in place plans and actions which would allow us to fulfill our dreams.

THE ITALIAN RIOTS-1952

Up until 1952, most of us who were at Bonegilla came from forced labour camps or other situations where we had been taken from our motherlands and were unable to return. We were homeless and displaced. We had come from situations where thousands of our people had died from starvation, forced depravation and loss of hope and liberty.

For us, Bonegilla provided us with safety, freedom, food, and the ability to once more hope and plan for a future which for so long had been denied us.

I loved our time at Bonegilla. However, by the middle of 1952, the atmosphere at Bonegilla had changed. The last of the displaced persons, (DPs) had come and now the new wave of people coming were assisted migrants. People from Italy and Holland who were able to pay part of their fare for their trip out here, were moving to Australia. They also had dreams for a better life. Often, they had borrowed money to come out here, planning to immediately go into paid employment when they arrived in Australia.

Australia was suffering an economic recession at this time, so these assisted migrants found themselves jobless and waiting for months on end for paid positions which simply did not eventuate as quickly as they wanted. Loans needing to be repaid were weighing heavily on them, especially the young and restless Italian men who were arriving during these years.

Adding to the unemployment problem, these people didn't accept or like the living conditions or the food which we had willingly accepted.

'You expect us to live in tin sheds!'

'We came from proper homes!'

'Even our animals had better housing than this!'

'And as for the toilets, they are disgusting!' they threw up their hands and shouted.

In the middle of 1952, employment officers could not find jobs outside of the camp for the first groups of assisted migrants from the United Kingdom, Netherlands, and Italy, and for the two hundred and eighty displaced persons still in residence, including us. We didn't mind. We both had jobs and our pickled cucumbers giving us an income. The Italian migrants minded very much, and the war cry went out, 'Give us jobs or repatriate us.'

By the beginning of 1952, Mykola and I were both working in the kitchen. The Italians hated the food,

'What's this stuff? That's not how you cook pasta.'

'We don't want your rissoles'

'Or your carrots'

'We want spaghetti'

And so, the complaints mounted. We became very nervous in the kitchen, not knowing how to cope with their anger. Some of the cooks resigned from the kitchen. I went to the camp director. 'I am scared of these people. I want to work, but I'm afraid in the kitchen.'

'Ludmila, we have the International Ball coming up soon, will you stay till that is over? We need you in the kitchen.'

'Alright, but I don't like it.', so I remained and helped prepare food for the ball. The ball came and went. The Italians were becoming increasingly vocal until finally in July, the unrest erupted into a full-, scale riot. The ball which we had worked so hard for, should have been the highlight of the year, but the riots completely overshadowed it.

THE ITALIAN RIOTS-1952

We noticed a noisy group building up. They were carrying rocks and placards. Those of us with children, gathered them up and hid in our respective homes. Wolodia began crying and Kola kept close to me. I barricaded my door with the table and chairs. Mykola as usual, was working in the kitchen. The noise and the shouting got louder, and we could hear things being smashed.

They damaged a lot of the buildings and streetlights. One man yelled, 'We ignito' and others rushed to join him, threatening to burn the camp down.

Kola held onto me, crying, as glass splintered somewhere nearby. I took hold of my boys, and we sat on the floor. I pulled the bedding over us to protect us from glass or rocks or anything else that may come through the windows. 'Please God, keep Mykola safe, keep us all safe.'

Police from Albury, Wodonga, Chiltern, and Wangaratta were rushed to the camp to bring law and order. An armed convoy from nearby Bandiana military barracks 'exercised' in the fields near Bonegilla for two hours. While they didn't enter Bonegilla, their visible presence helped to quieten the Italian men and stop the riot.

In August, the Italians began rioting three times a day at mealtimes.

Six hundred of them gathered up their plates of spaghetti and marched to the director's house. 'What do you call this?', they shouted, pointing at their spaghetti.

The director replied, 'I don't eat spaghetti, I will never eat spaghetti.'

All six hundred of them responded by throwing the food on the ground in front of the director's house. While the ball didn't get much attention, the riots made the front page of several newspapers.

Although the riots were frightening, they did bring about needed change.

Ethnic groups were housed together in their respective blocks.

Kitchens were built into the different ethnic blocks, so that the Italian chefs cooked for the Italians, Dutch chefs cooked for the Dutch.

Kitchens in the Italian blocks received special supplies of fish, macaroni, spaghetti, salt, tomato puree, olive oil, garlic, and coffee. The Dutch also received food requirements to meet their tastes, as did the Germans.

Deep latrines in some blocks were replaced by sewer systems,

canteens were lined and huts were painted.

Unemployed Italians were dispatched to ten-week emergency work positions, especially created for them within defence establishments.

Mykola continued to cook for the DPs but even our menus received an upgrade.

My request was met, when after the ball, the director approached me, 'Ludmila, would you like to work in the hospital?' For the remainder of 1952 and up until we left Bonegilla, eighteen months later, that is where I worked. I worked as a maid, cleaning, serving collecting meals, sometimes helping the nurses. During this time, I learnt much, such as how to fold and use a sling, how to treat burns, how to calm a frightened child. Much of what I learnt; I took into my day-to-day living.

The staff were all friendly. We had fun, we helped each other, and new friendships developed. I wore a sleeved dress or skirt and blouse with a full pinafore or apron over the top.

The hospital was pleasant, newly painted, with murals on the walls of the children's ward which had been painted by our Ukrainian friend, Paul, who had also decorated the creche. Lino covered the floors and ceiling fans cooled the rooms in the summer. The wards were now heated in the winter.

Our matron was efficient and kind. She wore a checked dress, and her white starched veil revealed her status and authority. She happily posed with us for staff photos. It was a comfortable, safe place to work. I no longer needed to fear riots while working there.

BEING UKRAINIAN

When we first arrived at Bonegilla, speaking in our own language was strongly discouraged. Learning to speak English was one of the main focuses of our being at Bonegilla. However, as time went by, the Australian authorities recognised the importance to us, of holding onto our own cultural identities. It became even more important to those of us who came from countries such as Ukraine, Poland, and the Baltic states where Russia and/or Germany had tried to obliterate our national culture, traditions, religion, language, and anything else that set us apart as being Ukrainian, Polish, or whatever ethnicity we belonged to.

We attended English classes and learnt to speak English, but in the privacy of our own huts or rooms, we spoke our own language and shared our own culture with each other. I was taken from my home and my family when I was very young, only two years old. When I was ten years old, I was put into a Russian Komsomol school and forced to speak Russian. German forced-labour camp sought to not just de-Ukrainianize me, but de-humanise me. I was regarded as sub-human, as were thousands of others. Despite this, my genetic code, or whatever it was, made me hold strongly to my nationality. I will be Australian, but I will forever be Ukrainian.

By 1952 we had established ethnic clubs and churches. We had our Ukrainian club and church. I loved the Ukrainian dance groups and the choral group. I took in everything Ukrainian that I could. What had been denied me as a child and teenager, I now hungrily devoured, soaking it up, like a thirsty plant absorbing water. I learnt our folksongs and our dances, and I clapped and cheered while our men danced and leaped their way through Cossack dances which had been forbidden during the rule of Stalin.

'Mutti, look', shouted Kola, as he imitated the older men, and little Wolodia joined in.

Russia and Nazi Germany denied God and forbade us to speak of or to worship God in our churches. Now, we had our own services and church. It was allowed and encouraged by Australia.

It was at Bonegilla that our own culture began to be put together again. As we held onto our own ethnic identities, it gave us the needed foundation and security to also reach out, grasp, and embrace our new Australian identity. I knew I could become both without giving up either.

NEW HORIZONS-1953

By the end of 1951, the last of the displaced persons had arrived at Bonegilla. From then on, only assisted migrants who paid part of their fare to come to Australia arrived at Bonegilla. The first of these migrants came from Italy and Holland.

Because so many of us had experienced terrible things at the hands of Nazi Germany, there was still a lot of resentment, fear and even hate amongst the displaced. 1953 saw the first big intake of Germans under the assisted programme.

Back in Germany, I had already made a German friend, in Frieda, who had helped hide and care for my baby while I was still a prisoner. Through her, I had learnt that not all Germans were cruel. I had also learnt that they too had suffered greatly during the war. I had learnt that not all Russians were hateful of us, and that they too ended up suffering a lot because of the war.

When the first Germans arrived, I was willing to accept them. It wasn't long before I met one special woman, just a little older than me. I was walking alone by the bank of the lake when I saw her. She was sitting on the grass, dabbing her eyes with her handkerchief. At first, I was going to walk past, but her sadness and her aloneness drew me to her. Sitting beside her, we began to talk,

'I am Ludmila'

'I am Ingrid', she replied. That was the beginning of us becoming 'best' friends.

By the end of 1953 news had come out, of work being available at a factory near Maitland in New South Wales. Ingrid and her husband, Fred applied for work there, were accepted and moved to Maitland.

We continued our friendship through writing letters to each other,

'Come, Ludmila, there is work here for both of you. There is another migrant camp at Greta, nearby. There are many from Ukraine and Germany. Courtauld's Rayon Factory is nearby.'

We made further enquiries. Courtaulds began building their factory at Tomago, close to the city of Maitland on the nineteenth of April 1950. It took three years for the factory to be complete. The factory produced yarns for motor tyres out of rayon and other synthetic fibres.

In 1953 they brought one hundred and fifty key workers from Britain to commence operations and to train others. They would be employing between 1500 and 2300 workers, who they would train to do the work at the factory.

LEAVING BONEGILLA 1953-1954

A letter came in the post with a photo of a house in Maitland,

'The house needs some loving, and you two could give it that. It is vacant, and you could afford it. It is not expensive.' Ingrid added a postscript, 'Please come, we miss you.'

It was enough. We applied to buy the house and we were accepted. Hugging each other, we, danced around our tiny space.

'We own a house in Australia. We are going to Maitland where we both have jobs waiting for us.'

We had been at Bonegilla for four years. During our time there, we had learnt to speak English, and how to use Australian money. We had both worked during those four years and had been able to save for a house, (or a deposit, at least). By the end of the year, Kola would be ten years old and Wolodia would be four and a half years old. He could begin school in 1955 making it easier for both Mykola and me to work at Maitland. We had nice clothes, and we were used to venturing into Albury/Wodonga for shopping expeditions. We felt ready to move into Australia, outside of Bonegilla which had provided a halfway home and protection for us in those first few years. Ingrid and Fred were urging us to join them in Maitland.

The boys weren't quite as eager. Another move, another school wasn't exactly what Kola wanted, but we knew it was the next move into our future. We pulled out our faithful, plywood chests and began packing.

While looking towards the future, I also took time to look back and reflect on the journey which had brought us here.

While waiting to board the boat which brought us here, I remember wandering through the narrow lanes of Naples and watching the local people living their lives. While children played in the streets, the adults sat around in circles on their chairs which they had brought out of their homes, to enjoy the sunshine and each other's company.

Wandering around Bonegilla, I watched as children played in the laneways between their huts while their parents sat around in circles on their chairs which they had brought out, enjoying the sunshine and each other's company.

Both experiences were so similar, albeit one was in Italy and the other in Australia. For us, both times were periods of waiting prior to us moving on to the next chapter of our lives. For me this realisation brought a sense of continuity and normality to our lives which in turn brought comfort. I went back to our little tin hut and completed the packing.

It was time to say, 'Goodbye Bonegilla, Australia, here we come.'

1950, Baby Wolodia born

Pig on the spit, Block 19 picnic, down near the lake.

First job At Bonegilla, working in the creche, 1950.
Ludmila is on the right.

Kitchen crew, Mykola centre front, Ludmila behind him to his right.

1950 Ludmila, Lake Hume, Bonegilla.

Ludmila and Mykola, Kitchen, 1951

Working in the hospital 1952-1954, Ludmila is far left.

Family photo, Bonegilla 1952.

PART 4
MAITLAND

1954- SETTLING IN TO WORK, SCHOOL, AND PLAY

MAITLAND FLOOD 1955

SUSIE'S BIRTH 1958

NATURALISATION

1965

ABORTION

RETURN TO UKRAINE

DEATH OF FATHER

NEW MEMORIES

THE LAST TEN YEARS

CAR ACCIDENT, HEADACHES AND HEARTACHE

MENTAL HOSPITAL

CANCER

MAITLAND 1954-SETTLING IN TO WORK, SCHOOL, AND PLAY

Weary and dishevelled after travelling by train all night from Albury, we stretched and looked around us. The train had slowed and was pulling into Maitland Railway Station. We woke the boys, gathered up our belongings and got ready to set foot in this place we would now call home. Fred and Ingrid met us, we collected our four big chests, loaded them onto the trailer and set off to see our house for the first time.

It was only minutes before we pulled up at 8 Grant St. It had been raining here for the last two months. The ground was soggy with puddles lying everywhere. The grass was long overdue for a mow, and it brushed, wet and sticky, against our legs. Without the sun, which was hidden behind thick clouds, the house appeared forlorn and weary. We were weary, and the combination of 'weary house' and 'weary us' dissolved the excitement we had built up and left us flat. The house was one street away from the main street, High Street, behind the town hall. The 1952 flood had gone through it, and since then, the house had stood vacant and neglected until we had bought it.

We turned the key in the front door and pushed it open. An unpleasant, damp, musty smell rushed out at us as we entered. Incongruous with the dampness outside, dust coated the house inside and cobwebs hung from the ceilings and in the corners of every room. The total emptiness of the house reverberated around us with its hollowness bouncing back from the naked walls, the undressed windows, and the bare wooden floors.

I had been so excited by the prospect of living in our very own home, that the grim reality of this forsaken sad house, slapped me in the face, and I felt hot tears trace down my cheeks.

'Oh, Mykola, what have we done?' Mykola shook his head as the realisation of what we had done, hit home.

"We should never have bought a house without first seeing it. I am so sorry Ludmila.'

Our belongings sat expectantly in the middle of the room. I rallied, 'Well, we are here now, and we must make it into our home. We can do it. Come, we need to buy a broom, bucket, mop, detergent, and eucalyptus oil.'

Soon, we gave Kola a broom and he set to work, getting rid of the cobwebs. Mykola swept the floors, and I followed him with the mop and bucket. Ingrid and Fred had arranged for the power to be turned on. The steamy hot water from the bucket, with the eucalyptus oil in it soon filled the rooms with the sweet scent of eucalyptus. We quickly unpacked our belongings and made the house into our home. We bought mattresses that day and laid them out on the now clean floors in the bedrooms and made the rooms welcoming with our bedlinen and covers. We placed our mats on the bare boards. What we had in our tin shed at Bonegilla didn't fill much of the space in the house. Still, it was a beginning.

The boys went to bed early, their eyes closing almost as soon as their heads touched the pillows. Eventually, we too climbed between the sheets. Running my hands over the mattress, feeling its newness and its thickness, I turned to Mykola, 'The mattress is so thick, it feels strange.'

'Mmm', replied Mykola, already half asleep. Worn out from the day's activities, my eyes closed, and we all slept the unbroken sleep of exhaustion.

The next morning, we woke to another wet day. We had breakfast, dressed, and with our umbrellas we made our way down onto the High Street and caught the bus to Courtauld's Rayon Factory where we were provided with our work clothes and rosters, ready to begin work the next week.

MAITLAND 1954-SETTLING IN TO WORK, SCHOOL, AND PLAY

Next stop was to the school to enrol our boys in their new school and buy uniforms for them, ready to begin school in the new year.

Back at our house, Mykola collected his garden fork and went into the backyard to begin digging a vegetable garden. The soil was saturated, and muddy water squelched all around him. The rain continued to fall. He put his tools away and came inside. Shaking his head, he raised his hands. 'Too wet'. The soil was so water-laden, that the vegetable garden had to wait.

Not long after, Mykola disappeared for about an hour. Then, I saw him coming through the front gate, umbrella in one hand, keeping the incessant rain off him and the other arm laden with parcels.

'Ludmila, look what I have!'. He put his load down on the verandah. 'Yesterday, I cleaned out the garden shed and found some tubs I can use to grow herbs in. Look, I have bought dill, mint, and basil and some lettuce and tomato plants. I can grow them in the tubs, and they won't get water-logged.'

I moved closer, 'Mykola, that is wonderful, and you have also bought some pansy plants to give us some colour.'

'Yes, we'll keep them on the verandah and look after them. It's not a lot, but it is something Ludmila'. So, despite the continual rain, we began our garden.

Fred and Ingrid visited later that day. Our boys joined their children and went out onto the verandah to play while we sat around the table, drinking coffee, and eating cake which Ingrid had baked and brought over to share with us.

'We both begin work next week, but we still don't know what to do with our boys while we are at work.' I looked at Ingrid, while without realising what I was doing, beat a nervous tattoo on the table with my fingers.

Ingrid reached across the table and placed her hand over mine.

'Ludmila, it's alright. Our boys will look after them.'

'Yes', interjected Fred, 'all the migrant kids meet up and look after each other.'

'When it is sunny, they go down to the river, which isn't far away, but when it is rainy like today, they meet up in each other's homes.' added Ingrid.

'Mind you, they have their chores to do before they meet up, but they are good kids and there has never been a problem, you'll see!'

So, I relaxed a little, wrote up a list of chores for the boys, organised their lunches and went to work. The first few days, I still worried, but as the days and weeks continued, I stopped fretting, knowing my children were safe and happy. We would come home, shower and then relax around the dinner table, sharing stories of our day with each other.

'We found this big, old willow tree.'

'With branches over the water.'

'Yes, so thick and strong, we could swing ourselves out into the river.'

'We'd see who could jump out the furthest.'

Another day, the boys had a different skill which they shared. Kola began,

'Today, Ivor showed us how to skim rocks across the water' Wolodia, pretending to skim stones, added his bit,

'We had to find flat stones.'

'Yes, and then we would flick them so that they'd spin across the water like this,' and we would get a double demonstration on the skill of skimming stones.

'Alexi got the furthest. His rock just kept skimming across the water.'

MAITLAND 1954–SETTLING IN TO WORK, SCHOOL, AND PLAY

Another day, we came home and found a jar containing tadpoles taking centre stage on our dining room table.

'See! they have legs.'

'And soon they'll lose their tails.'

'And then they will be frogs.'

With this information, the tadpoles/frogs soon found themselves exiled to the garden pond and forbidden entrance inside the house.

Just before Christmas, Courtaulds hosted a Christmas party for its workers, at the bowling club which was across the road from the factory. The tables were laden with food, and the best part for the children was the arrival of Santa Claus. With his snowy white beard, big belly, and bright red suit, he would arrive with much fanfare and bags of gifts for the children. As each child's name was called out, the children, some boisterous, some fearful or shy, received their gifts. That Christmas, Kola received a book of stories and a bright blue toy car. Wolodia received a set of matchbox cars and a colouring-in-book and pencils.

Our first Christmas in Maitland came just weeks after we had arrived, but Mykola found us a tree and we all joined in, decorating it, and putting presents under the tree. Mykola made a Christmas pudding and together we made cabbage rolls, piroshki and other Ukrainian dishes to put on our table. I put a jar of our pickled cucumbers, which I had bottled back at Bonegilla on the table. We picked lettuce and tomatoes from our own garden (albeit in tubs)

and celebrated our first Christmas in Maitland.

Courtauld's factory was built on flat ground which had been asphalted to form a large carpark. The factory itself, consisted of many multi-storeyed brick buildings. A very tall chimney rose into the air, belching out clouds of smoke, providing a very visible landmark which could be seen for miles around.

The Hunter River flowed past nearby, spanned by the Hexham Bridge, which was constructed in 1952 to replace the punt, a pulley-drawn raft which people used to drive their vehicles onto, and be pulled across the river.

Inside the buildings, were vast rooms full of huge looms and machinery which produced strong rayon thread. The machinery, when in operation was extremely noisy. We would rise early in the morning and walk twenty minutes to Melbourne Street where we would board the bus and be at work by 6.00 a.m. Work would finish at 3.30 and we would catch the bus back to Melbourne St. and walk the short distance back home.

Christmas came and went and by the end of January, it was time for the boys to begin school.

'Mykola, we need to give Wolodia an English/Australian name.'

'Yes, I agree.'

'Kola is alright, it is like Colin but what can we call Wolodia?'

'We call him Lodia for short, so let's call him Walter.'

'Yes, that sounds good.'

So, when they went to school, they were Kola and Walter.

Another little girl whose parents were both Ukrainian named their daughter Margaret, after Princess Margaret. Once she began school, her name was shortened to 'Margie'.

Most of the people living in our street were new Australians, so the Australians called our street 'Wog St, and called us wogs.

Because all the adults worked at Courtaulds and left for work by 5.30 in the morning, all our children or 'kids' walked to school. At first, it was them and us; the Aussies or the British- 'them', and 'us', the wogs.

The first day at school, Walter forgot his lunch and cried but Kola shared his lunch with him, and they both got through the day.

Margie's mum had made her salami sandwiches. They smelt and the Aussie kids tormented her,

'Stinky Wog', 'stinky food'.

From that day on her mum would make her the salami sandwiches and Margie would throw them away on the way to school. Being hungry was better than being different and teased.

While both Kola and Walter knew enough English to get by, Margie didn't know a word of English when she began school. However, children learnt quickly and soon made up for their shortfall in the English language.

Maitland had a large proportion of non-English-speaking students because of the Courtaulds factory and the nearby migrant camp. The schools needed to cater to this demographic.

At Maitland Primary School, a buddy system was introduced, where an Australian child would sit next to a migrant child to befriend and help newcomers. Sometimes it worked, sometimes it didn't.

The children had to speak English at school. Initially, this was a huge hurdle for many children.

Not only was language a barrier, but other things caused barriers as well. The migrant or displaced children were not as wealthy as their Australian counterparts.

Having relatives; aunts and uncles, grandparents, or not having these relatives, also helped to separate the 'haves' and the 'have-nots'.

Nevertheless, children are curious, and this curiosity built solid bridges and lasting friendships were formed. We had an Australian family across the road, as did lots of migrant families.

The Aussies loved Ukrainian or German or Polish or whatever nationality's food, while the migrants loved the Aussie food, so Ukrainian piroshki and cabbage rolls, British fish and chips, Italian pizzas and Aussie meat pies were exchanged or shared as the Aussies and migrants learnt how to mingle and accept each other.

The Ukrainian kids had to go to the Catholic school for two hours on Saturdays to learn to read and write Ukrainian. The Ukrainian kids balked at this and soon stopped going,

'Why do we have to go. We are in Australia now. We want to be Aussies.'

During the long hot summers and in the holidays, after the children had completed their homework and chores, they would often go down to the dump, which was close by. They would collect whatever they could to make billycarts for themselves and race them. Wooden boxes, disused lawnmowers and pram wheels, bits of rope and anything which could be used was recycled.

Walter and his little friend, Margie tried to make a kite one day. They joined together a cross frame of fence palings, covered it with paper, attached a rope and launched it into the sky. It didn't stay airborne at all and took an immediate nosedive.

'Run!' shouted Walter, and sprinted, with Margie right behind him. The kite hit the ground. They tried again and again, but the wood was way too heavy for a kite. Their dream that day took a nosedive along with the kite but didn't die.

'We'll look for some cane and try again', Margie rolled up her paper to take home, ready for the next kite.

'Hey, you two, are you up for a game of rounders, shouted another boy, and soon, kite forgotten for then, two teams were soon formed. They hit their rag ball and ran from base to base, laughing and competing against each other until it was time to go home.

MAITLAND 1954–SETTLING IN TO WORK, SCHOOL, AND PLAY

It wasn't just the children who face struggles and rejection as new Australian residents. Now that we were in our new wide world which for us was Australia, without the protective cloak of Bonegilla Migrant Camp, we too felt the barbs of racism. We always caught the bus at the same place each morning and got off at the same place in the evening when our day's work was done. However, we heard of instances with friends who were victimised.

Alexi was ropeable when he told Mykola, 'The bus driver drove right past my stop even though I was standing ready to get off. He kept driving until he stopped quite a distance away, outside the home of an Australian. Rain or shine, it made no difference. He would not pull up and let me off at my bus stop.'

I remember times when I would go to the shop and stand in queue to pay and had to wait until the cashier had served the Australian people behind me first. Only when they were all served, would she serve me. It could have been that she was as uncomfortable with our lack of English, as we were. However, it felt as though these people were treating us as though we were subhuman, as they did when in Germany under nazi rule, or in Ukraine under Stalin. Those instances were thankfully in the minority. As time progressed, our language improved, we got to know each other and communication between us improved.

Not long after arriving in Maitland, a Ukrainian Club was formed. Nearby was another migrant camp at Greta. We hired a hall at Greta, eventually purchasing it, and we used it regularly for church meetings, dances, dinners, and celebrations. Very soon, we were part of a thriving fun-filled and supportive group.

MAITLAND FLOOD 1955

I woke early to the sound of heavy rain drumming on the roof. Rain on the roof was more the norm than sunshine since we moved here nearly four months ago. Incessant rain, influenced by a la Nina since October 1954 had saturated the land. It was Wednesday, 23rd of February. It was a workday for Mykola and me and school for the boys. As the day progressed, the rain became heavier. As I worked at my loom, I fretted about our house and belongings. When we arrived home, I voiced my fear,

'Mykola, I think we should pack some of our things in case it floods.'

Upending one of our crates which we'd covered with a cloth, and was using as a table, Mykola began to gather our things. Before we went to bed, we had packed our most precious belongings in readiness, should we have to move. During the night the rain increased. The boys slept through the night, but Mykola and I paced the house, frequently looking outside to see if we could see floodwater approaching towards us. Eventually we slept a broken, fitful sleep.

It seemed as though we had just closed our eyes when we heard knocking at the door. Opening it, we were met by two men in raincoats and gumboots. It was Thursday, 24th February.

'Ma'am, Sir, we are letting you know that you must prepare to be evacuated. Floodwater is rising right across the valley. Trucks will be coming to help you move to safe ground.' With that, they continued onto the next houses along our street. Waking the boys, we packed everything into our chests and suitcases.

Between 1949 and 1955, Maitland had been flooded eight times to varying degrees. Maitlanders had become experts at neighbourhood level self-help endeavours. Groups of men would move from house to house, moving furniture to drays and trucks and taking the loaded trucks to East Maitland and Telarah, both suburbs on high ground which were not affected by the floods, where the furniture and trunks would be stored safely in buildings there.

We were only new to Maitland but became part of this amazing self-help programme. I packed clothes and essentials in a separate bag for us to take with us to wherever we would be evacuated.

Courtaulds closed production and secured the factory as best they could.

Torrential rain caused flights to be cancelled at nearby, Williamtown Airport.

An emergency was declared, and the council began preparing for evacuation.

Our neighbours across the road came over to tell us,

'Muswellbrook, just north of us in the Upper Hunter Valley is flooded.'

We turned on our radio to glean more information. The radio boomed out, 'The mail train has crashed into floodwaters at Togar, in the Hunter Valley, just below Muswellbrook.'

'All this water in the Upper Hunter will soon reach us', our neighbour warned. These neighbours had gone through the last floods. Our anxiety rose another level but that night we again stayed in our packed-up home as the floodwaters came closer. We pulled the boys mattresses into our room, and we slept together that night.

On Friday, the 25th [of] February the Hunter River began to overflow into the Maitland suburb of Bolwarra, only three and a half miles (four or five kilometres) away.

The main bridge, The Belmont Bridge closed at 8.30 a.m. and a full-scale evacuation of the city began. We were told to keep our radios on for further news and instructions.

At 11.00 a.m. the Mayor of Maitland warned us of an approaching wall of water as the first levee failure occurred at Oakhampton, only about three kilometres from where we lived. As the levee broke and the wall of water rushed through Oakhampton, homes were instantly ripped from their foundations.

We were evacuated and taken to The Currency Hotel in High Street where we were given an upstairs room. By nightfall, water was two metres deep on the city main street, High Street. Our house was only one street away. Water swept through the lower level of the hotel, and we stood at the window, watching our world disappear under the murky, savage floodwaters. During the night floodwaters roared through Maitland and our home.

While we and our belongings were safe, there were many people who had not left their homes when it was safe to do so. The next day, Saturday the, 26th of February, Australian army ducks, (amphibious vehicles) and surf-lifesaving surfboats rescued over one thousand people, many of them stranded on rooftops.

That day, a Royal Australian Navy helicopter, while on a rescue mission hit powerlines. Four people who were dangling on a rope suspended from the helicopter were electrocuted. The helicopter spun, crashed, and exploded, killing the two crew inside the helicopter.

Several cars, a double-decker bus and two hundred people managed to get onto the High St. bridge and became stranded there. A young twenty-year-old volunteer of St. John's Ambulance and one police officer were taken to the bridge in an army duck. Those people remained stranded there for fourteen days. The upper deck of the bus became sleeping quarters, and the lower deck was used as a first-aid centre. During that time the stench of dead carcases floating down the river or stuck in the mud, and the continual onslaught of mosquitos made life on that bridge almost unbearable.

On Sunday, 27th of February, thousands of homeless refugees were taken to Greta migrant camp and homes all over the Hunter Valley. 4,000 food parcels were dropped by the Royal Australian Airforce.

By Monday, the 28th of February, the water began to subside, leaving behind a thick blanket of putrid silt and debris. As areas began to emerge from the floodwaters, clean-up began.

After the flood, we, as individuals, and corporately, began to take stock of what had happened and of our losses.

An extremely intense monsoonal depression had formed over Southeast Queensland on the 23rd of February and moved south, dumping the highest rainfall amounts since 1885 (seventy years), with rainfalls exceeding two hundred millimetres or eight inches.

The record height of a Maitland flood was exceeded by nearly a metre. Some homes were flooded with as much as five metres of muddy water. 15,000 people were evacuated, mostly by boat or helicopter. Thirty-one homes were never rebuilt.

The flood overwhelmed rivers on both sides of the Great Dividing Range, creating an inland sea the size of England and Wales combined.

The worst hit was Maitland, which was sited on low-lying land along the Hunter River. The city was completely inundated by floodwaters. A total of twenty-five lives were lost during a week of flooding. The flood washed away fifty-eight homes and damaged one hundred and three homes beyond repair. In Maitland alone, 2,180 houses were flooded.

We stood on the footpath, outside our home. Thick, putrid mud coated everything. Looking towards the house, my eyes were drawn to the dirty line which showed us how high the water had risen. Stifling a sob, I pointed to the guttering, 'Look, Mykola, the whole house, up to the roof went under.'

Taking the key, Mykola turned it and pushed the door open. That horrible, stinking mud coated the floors, the walls, and the windows. Absolutely everything was covered in silt; brown, thick, and smelling like nothing I had ever smelt before. I recoiled in horror, stepping back outside the door, covering my nose to try and block out the sickening smell.

'Well, we have survived the starvation regime of Stalin, the brutality of Hitler's forced-labour camps and the bombing raids. We will get through this also.'

Clad in gumboots, rubber gloves and scarves over our noses, we picked up our hoses, brooms, spades, and disinfectant, and began the job of reclaiming our home from the devastation caused by the flood.

Over the next few weeks, the house was restored, the garden began to look like a garden once more and life returned to its normal routine. We were so thankful for the Maitlander teams who had moved all our belongings, including our furniture.

A couple of weeks after the flood, we were approached by the bank informing us that they too had been flooded in High Street, and they had lost all their records. Because of this they informed us that we would have to pay for the house again.

'No, we won't!', I went to the bank with my receipt of payment,

'See, here is our proof of payment.' I took all our documents with me when we were evacuated. 'We don't owe you anything.' And that was the end of the matter. My receipt was proof of payment and could not be disputed. We were safe.

SUSIE'S BIRTH 1958

Towards the end 0f 1957, I felt the tell-tale signs of pregnancy again. We began gathering baby things once more, ready to welcome our new little baby. Already having our two beautiful sons, we secretly hoped that this time we would be blessed with a baby girl. Kola was nearly thirteen and Walter was nine years old. I continued to work as I had with my first two pregnancies and things seemed to be progressing normally. Then, far too early in the pregnancy, I felt the pain associated with birth.

'Mykola, I'm having our baby, we have to get to the hospital.'

Mykola got me into a taxi, and we hurried to the hospital. Not long after, I gave birth to our precious baby.

'You have a daughter', I was told as they hurried her away. I didn't even see her. What should have been a time of joy, turned into one of fear. She was very premature and weighed only two pounds, (.9 of a kilo). She was so tiny, that I couldn't even nurse her. We named her Suzanne and prayed that she would survive and thrive. Her weight, already tiny, plummeted to one pound and nine ounces. When I was able to see her, she looked so fragile. She was wrapped in cotton wool and was on oxygen, while she lay in her humidicrib. She remained in the humidicrib for three months. I couldn't hold her or touch her or feed her. Mykola held me as I sobbed. Soon, I was allowed to go home. It was so strange. I had a baby, yet, I didn't have a baby. I desperately wanted to hold her, but I could only look at her. With everything in me, I willed for my Suzie, my daughter, to live. Suzie was born on the 28th of January 1958.

A team of ten nurses, led by a sister Dobb, fed her with one drop of brandy and ten drops of milk every hour from an eye dropper. Every day, I expressed milk from my breasts and Mykola walked with it to the hospital where it was given to Suzie. I loved her so much but was being eaten up by fear that I would lose her. I was afraid to bond with her and then lose her, so chose to stay home. As she began to gain weight, my fear began to subside, and I was able to go with Mykola and see my precious Suzie. I know some people would have condemned me, but I did what I could, and dealt with my fear in the only way I could.

When Suzie was three months old, she was able to be in a normal crib and we could at last nurse her and bond with her. Suzie remained in the hospital until she was five months old. Then, wrapped warmly in a shawl, for it was now winter, we took her home. We could now show off our special, tiny daughter. She was like a newborn. Thanks to the nursing staff and Suzie's will to live, she survived and grew. We were now a proud family of five.

NATURALISATION

After we brought Suzie home, I began thinking a lot about my family back in the Ukraine. I was only two when I was removed from our home, and our family was torn apart. My mother had died. I knew that. I was with her when she passed away from starvation during Stalin's regime. My father had been taken by the Russians, and that was all I knew. Did he survive, and if he did, where is he now.

For years there had been no communication between families in the Ukraine and the diaspora of Ukrainians scattered across the world. Fear of repercussions was a huge barrier. Another barrier was miscommunication. Ukrainians in the homeland had been told that their loved ones were traitors who were working for the enemy. Then when those same ones, believed to be traitors, went to other lands, like us in Australia, questions were asked, 'Why didn't they come back and help rebuild our country, Ukraine?' The families in Ukraine didn't know that we were not allowed to go back.

Fear, mistrust, and miscommunication separated families for twenty or thirty years.

In the late fifties someone wrote back to family in Ukraine, and communication was made without adverse consequences. Through family and village networking in Ukraine, and likewise, here in Australia and other countries the broken tapestry of families began to be rewoven. Letters, information, and gifts began to be exchanged. A friend received a parcel from her father in Ukraine, a small hand-made wooden box containing three small bottles of perfume.

Shipping and postal costs were expensive. Then one of our Ukrainian friends suggested,

'Why don't we communally buy a crate. We can all put our gifts in it, and when it is full, ship it back to Ukraine. We share the cost. It will be cheaper than sending everything individually.'

'What a great idea', and I set about gathering up gifts, photos, and letters to add to the crate. The idea quickly took hold and communication between our countries flourished.

Word finally came through that my father was alive and had returned to his village. I desperately wanted to return to the Ukraine, see my father and other relatives and reconnect with my roots, but to do that, I needed a passport. To get a passport I needed to become a naturalised Australian.

I got the application forms and filled them out:

Full name

Native Place

Occupation

Age

Date and Ship of Arrival

Over 16 years of Age

Good Character

I had to have an adequate knowledge of my responsibilities and privileges as a citizen,

English language abilities,

Knowledge and understanding of Australian society, virtues, and history. (That included a knowledge of cricket! I learnt all the Australian champion bowlers and batsmen).

Intent to reside and work in Australia.

There were three privileges I especially wanted and would have when I became an Australian citizen:

NATURALISATION

*I could get an Australian passport and be able to re-enter Australia

freely.

*If I needed it, I could obtain help from an Australian official while overseas, (especially relevant if I needed help while in Ukraine).

*Registering children born overseas as Australian citizens by descent.

While Walter and Suzie were born in Australia and as such were Australian citizens, Kola was only thirteen and born in Germany in a forced labour camp. He would be included on my naturalization Certificate and because he never had a birth certificate, the Naturalization Certificate with his name on it could be used instead, whenever he needed a birth certificate.

On the 5th of February 1959, Mykola, and I with our children beside us, swore allegiance to Her Majesty Queen Elizabeth Second, in front of a photo of the Queen, the British Union Jack and the Australian flag. We officially became fully fledged Australian citizens.

The next things on my agenda were to apply for a passport and save up for the airfare to Ukraine.

1965

After the 1955 flood, Maitland put in place a flood mitigation programme. Over the next fifteen years they built one hundred and eighty-five kilometres of levee and control banks, nearly four kilometres of spillways, one hundred and sixty-five kilometres of drainage channels, two hundred and fifty-nine floodgates and thirty-six kilometres of bank protection works. The levees and controlled floodways protect the city from minor to moderate floods. Maitland's floodways divert major flows in a controlled manor around the city.

Even as the council put in place a plan to safeguard the city of Maitland, we too put a plan in place to safeguard us from future floods. Just as it took years to implement the council plans, so too did it take years for us to bring our plan to fruition. While we continued to live in the flood prone, Grant Street house, we began exploring the suburbs of East Maitland and Telara which were built on the hills and would never flood. We knew how to save, and we handled our finances carefully. We began building another nest egg to buy another home when the time was right. Mykola established a productive vegetable garden which saved us money. We continued to make and sell our pickled cucumbers.

We walked miles, looking at houses and building sites.

'Ludmila, what about this block?' Mykola pointed to the block we were standing in front of, in East Maitland.

'Yes, it's perfect' and we signed the contract for a block of land in Thompson St. East Maitland.

We began looking at house plans and eventually, ten years later, we sold the house in Grant St. We moved into our brand-new house on the hill in 1965. It smelt new and glistened. It would never flood. We would be safe. The outside weatherboard walls were sparkling white. The walls inside were in soft, clean colours, the floors were covered with lino in the living areas and carpet in the lounge and bedrooms. The kitchen, with its brand-new stove/oven was a dream come true. We bought a new lounge and dressed the windows with new curtains and blinds. Mykola took me in his arms, and we danced through our house. I felt like a princess moving into her castle.

Not long after moving into our beautiful new home, we bought our first car, a brand new, EJ Holden, light green with a white roof. Kola was now twenty, Walter was fifteen and Suzie was seven.

Since being taken away from us when I was two, my father had spent many years in the forced labour camps of the Russian/Stalin regime. Food rations had barely kept him alive, and his ragged clothes were insufficient to keep him warm during the long severe winters. Somehow, my father had survived. Most of the people who had been taken to the gulags died there.

The last communication we had, told me that although Papa had survived, those long years of being in the Siberian Gulags had taken a huge toll on his body.

'Mykola, I must go back and see him before it is too late.

'You don't have your passport yet, Ludmila.'

'No, but I have filled out the forms and paid for it. It must arrive in the mail soon.'

ABORTION

Mykola hugged me, and we continued to get ready for work that morning. I hadn't eaten any breakfast because I was feeling sick. I didn't tell anyone and went to work. The next day, I again felt nauseous, and I knew I was pregnant.

When I came home from work, the mail was sitting on the kitchen bench, where the boys had put it. I flicked through the envelopes till my eyes rested on an official looking letter. I felt it. It had a thicker 'something' in it. I opened the envelope and pulled out a small booklet. It was my passport.

'Mykola, I have my passport, look!' I waved it in the air, 'and I have enough money for the return airfare.'

I was going to Ukraine, and I was planning to go for three months.

'But don't you need a visa to stay that long?'

'Yes, I will apply for it.'

I received the application form and began to fill it in. I was also coming into the third month of my pregnancy and soon I would not be able to hide it anymore. It was February. I planned to go to the Ukraine for the summer, which was from June till the end of August.

I knew I had a problem. Feeling my stomach and knowing that a new baby was growing in there, I knew I had to make a very hard decision. If I had this baby, I would never see my father, for his health was failing rapidly. The baby was due at the end of August. If I had my baby in the Ukraine, then I feared the authorities would forcibly take my baby from me, claiming that the baby born in Ukraine, was Ukrainian by birth. Secondly, I had to declare if I was pregnant on the visa application because

I would be billeted for the three months. Lastly, I would not be able to fly anyway in my third trimester.

'Mykola, I am pregnant', I told him, forcing back tears.

'Yes, I had guessed you were.'

"But I want to see my father, and I will have to abort our baby to go and see him. What should I do?'

Mykola held me tightly, as I fought with my emotions, 'Whatever you decide, I will stand beside you.'

Neither of us slept that night, but by morning, I had made my decision. I would go back to the Ukraine and see my father. I had battled with my dilemma. Why did I have to choose between my father and my unborn child. I had done everything possible to save the life of my first-born son in the German forced-labour camp. I had lived in terrible fear that my daughter would die when she was in hospital for those five months, fighting for her life. Now I was consciously ending the life of this, my fourth child. I had the abortion and I cried for weeks after, mourning for the loss of that little life.

I filled in the visa application and sent it off. The visa arrived in due course. All I needed now was the plane ticket.

RETURN TO UKRAINE

In the months leading up to my trip, I made lists of what to take with me. There were two main items that were requested from the people in Ukraine: money, and embroidery thread. I was only allowed to take a certain amount of money with me by law.

'Sew it into the hems of your clothes', one of my friends told me, so little by little, I folded notes and carefully lined my hems.

Embroidery thread was impossible to get in the Ukraine. Embroidery was something most of the women did. It was part of their culture. Their clothes, especially their national costumes had a lot of embroidery decorating the clothes. I wanted to take some thread with me. If I packed it in my bag, customs were sure to take a lot of it. Then the same friend reiterated her original suggestion. 'Sew it into the hems of your clothes.' I collected a lot of embroidery threads in many different colours. I unpicked the hem of my coat and painstakingly sewed the threads into the lining. I would use tiny stitches the length of the coat, then without cutting the thread, stitched back along the hem, repeating the process until the thread was all sewn in. Then I would get another colour and repeat the process. With wide hems, I could get several lengths of cotton into a hem. My skirts received the same treatment. Being sewn into the lining, the stitching was not visible upon inspection. I wore one of my skirts and my coat onto the plane when I left for Ukraine.

Arriving in Ukraine and then travelling to Kamiana, I listened to all the chatter around me. Trying to listen to and answer their questions, while looking from side to side, taking in the views of this my native country was exciting, happy, sad, overwhelming. How could all these emotions be inside me at the same time? It was like being in a blender, mixing all the faces, the scenes, the conversations, the questions, and my emotions into one big unfathomable whole which I then wanted to separate out into their respective units. Exhaustion from this very long journey didn't help. I needed a sleep. Tomorrow, I could begin processing this strange but wonder-filled experience.

DEATH OF FATHER

During the summer, families congregated together. I met cousins and distant relatives, none of which I knew. Over the days, weeks and months, the jigsaw of my family began to come together.

The biggest piece of the jigsaw was missing. My father had died before I got there. The emotion of crying for my father who I only vaguely remembered was a strange emotion. I grieved not so much for who I knew and had lost but I grieved for who I had lost but had never had the chance to really know. Nevertheless, the grief I experienced was very real.

A relative pointed across to a woman with a group of people around her,

'That woman is Mykola's first wife', then pointing out three other people next to her, 'and they are his three children.'

I looked at them and looked away, but my eyes were drawn back to them repeatedly.

'He thought they were dead. He didn't think they would survive after he was captured.' I stammered, 'What should I do.'

'Nothing, it's alright, they know about and your children. It was a long time ago and it was during the war.'

'Yes, twenty-three years ago since we were forcibly taken from Ukraine.'

NEW MEMORIES

Over the next three months, I gathered new memories to take home. As we unpicked the hems of my clothes and took out the treasured embroidery threads and money, we exchanged stories of each other's lives and re-joined some of the broken threads of our family's rich tapestry.

I walked barefoot on the grassy verge of the creek and waded in the water, feeling the soil of my homeland squelching between my toes. Lying in bed at night and looking up at the stars, I reacquainted myself with the northern hemisphere's night sky.

'Ooh, I remember this scent', I breathed as the aroma of the crushed herbs below my feet reached my nostrils. Bending down, I gathered up a handful and held it to my face. Marietta laughed, and reaching up, shook the branches of the Tilia trees till they too, released their citrus fragrance. The oak trees had an abundance of acorns, still green but beginning to turn golden as they ripened.

I immersed myself in the bubbly, happy chatter, and culture of my people. Their poverty and the visible evidence of what they had endured provided a stark contrast to the happy abandonment of our laughter. They had suffered as much, if not more than I had. The realisation sobered me and formed in me an even tighter bond with these, my people, and my homeland.

The three months passed quickly, and it was time to return home to Australia. My suitcases were packed with gifts for my family back home. I had bought Mykola an electric shaver, Ukrainian embroidered clothes for us all, embroidered pillowcases and three bottles of Vodka.

I also bought several embroidered golden tryzubs, set against our Ukrainian blue background and surrounded by sheaves of wheat and our native wildflowers. Back home they would be framed and hung on our walls. This embroidery depicted our Ukrainian coat-of-arms.

The tryzub is the Ukrainian trident, the ancestral sign of the Rurik dynasty of the tenth to twelfth centuries, Kyivan Rus. Its image has been found on coins, seals, utensils, bricks, and murals. In the tenth century, the obverse side of coins during the rule of Volodymyr the Great, Prince of Kyiv, bore his portrait. The other side of the coins, the trident was depicted as Volodymyr's symbol of power.

In 1918, after the collapse of the Russian Empire, the Ukrainian People's Republic approved the tryzub as the Ukrainian coat-of-Arms. I took them home, distributed them and valued them as powerful reminders of our Ukrainian heritage.

THE LAST TEN YEARS

By 1969 my boys had grown into young men.

Kola studied accountancy and set off to see the world. He flew to Africa, getting a position as an accountant/ auditor in Rhodesia (Zimbabwe) which enabled him to travel to several African countries as he audited different companies throughout the continent. He loved the wildness of both the country and its wildlife; lions, elephants, zebras, and the many other animals there.

Walter had fallen in love with his childhood playmate, Margie. I was thrilled. Margie was Ukrainian and I couldn't have been happier. Walter was training as an engineer and Margie was training as a nurse. They were respectively nineteen and eighteen and married as teenagers, as did I, all those years ago. The end of that year, our first grandchild was born, a little girl. I was forty-two and a grandmother. Life was looking good. We bought another block of land, high on the hill in Brisbane St. and built a two-storey brick home on it. In 1970 we moved into that house and sold the Thompson St. house to Walter and Margie.

CAR ACCIDENT, HEADACHES AND HEARTACHE

Not long after moving into Brisbane St, I learnt to drive and got my licence. It was another big milestone in my life, giving me more freedom and independence. Life was not just good. It was very good, almost too good to be true.

One day Mykola and I went for a drive and were returning home. I was driving. I turned off the New England Highway into Brisbane Street, when I was hit by a car which had pulled out of a carpark, hitting us hard. I had been knocked out. Mykola had to get glass picked out of his head, and our car was written off.

The driver of the other car accused me of being at fault. He stated that I had hit him. I knew that I hadn't. We were in a stalemate situation. It was impossible and we didn't know what to do when a witness came forward and gave a statement

'I saw the accident. He pulled out of a parking space, where he always parks, (I come this way all the time). He pulled out without looking and hit her as she was driving past.'

The charge against me was dropped, he was charged, and his insurance company paid us for our destroyed car. Mykola's headwounds soon healed and we both went back to work.

Not long after, while at work, I felt this headache grip my head. I called over the supervisor, and went and sat down, holding my head in my hands. I went home early.

'Maybe, I'm getting the flu', I told my family and climbed into bed. It wasn't flu, but the headaches persisted and steadily got worse. I tried to get by with painkillers.

1974, Kola brought home a young woman with long black hair. She was a music teacher, but she was not Ukrainian

'Kola, why don't you marry a Ukrainian girl?'

'Because I love Marion, Mum.'

I really wanted him to marry a girl from my beloved country, so I kept introducing Ukrainian girls to him, but he wouldn't budge. He loved this girl, and she was lovely, just not Ukrainian. Three months after meeting her they became engaged. I accepted her as part of the family and stopped trying to marry him off to someone else. I didn't tell him about the headaches, and six months later, went to their wedding at Tamworth, about three and a half hours drive away.

The headaches were becoming more frequent and quite severe. I went to several doctors, but they dismissed me. They thought I was playacting to get a payout from the car accident.

Kola and Marion had a little boy, Timothy, my first grandson, in June 1975. I love my grandchildren. Then, late in 1976, Kola packed up his family and moved to the bottom of Tasmania. I had to let them go.

'But, why so far away?'

It broke my heart. In January 1976 they had a little girl, Tabitha. I saw photos but could not hold her.

I went to many doctors and specialists but received no answers. The headaches we're becoming unbearable, I was losing the ability to speak, and I was becoming increasingly depressed. Parts of my legs were becoming numb.

When you don't get answers to your problem, you will try anything and everything. I went to an acupuncturist. While on the table, I had a seizure and blood came out of my nose and mouth. He told Mykola to take me home. Mykola carried me to the car and did as he was told. We were both overwhelmed and didn't know what to do next.

MENTAL HOSPITAL

We kept going to different doctors. Eventually, one doctor told us that I had a mental problem and admitted me into the Watt St. Mental Hospital. I knew I didn't have a mental problem. I picked up my handbag and belted the doctor across the head. I fought them, but they were too strong for me, and I was admitted. I became more depressed but could do nothing. By this time, I couldn't speak.

I managed to escape from Watt St and ran away but I guess they were used to people escaping. They found me and took me back and ensured that I couldn't escape again.

CANCER

After about a month there, a doctor from Watt St, after testing me, rang Walter and Margie.

'Your mother does not have a mental problem. You need to come and get her and have a brain scan done.'

I was taken to the Royal North Shore hospital in Sydney where the scan revealed a brain tumour.

Margie hugged me. 'Mum, they are going to operate on your head and then you'll be alright, and you will be able to go back home.' I was so happy. I smiled at her and gave a thumbs up sign.

The hospital staff prepared me and took me down to theatre. The operation was supposed to have taken many hours.

My family went into the chapel to wait and pray. In the meantime, the hospital did another scan. They never did operate. The tumour had grown hugely in that short time since the last scan. They transferred me back to Maitland from Sydney.

Soon after, Kola, Marion and my two grandchildren arrived from Tasmania. I was able to hold and cuddle them both, Tabitha for the first time.

A few days later, I was admitted into Maitland hospital. Margie bought me a beautiful white, smocked summer nightdress for me to wear. It was very beautiful, with tiny pink flowers and soft green leaves embroidered on it. I pointed to the drawer beside my bed, indicating for her to put it there.

After Margie had left, I rolled over on to my side and clenched my fists. I had won so many battles, but I knew this was one battle I could not win. I also realised I would not see my family again.

LUDMILA

Ludmila passed away on the 15th of January 1978 aged fifty years. When she was laid to rest, she was dressed in that beautiful white nightdress.

CANCER

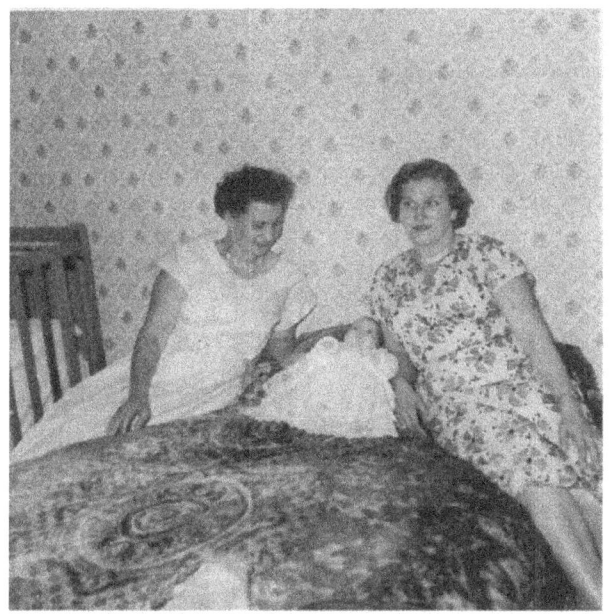

Ludmila and friend with baby Suzie, home after first five months in hospital.

Mykola watched by Ludmila and Suzie in their vege garden.

Ludmila receiving flowers for her birthday from Mykola.

The children, Woladia, Kola and Suzie.

A LETTER TO LUDMILA
(Written by Marion, her daughter-in-law)

Dear Ludmila,

You passed away far too soon. I only knew you for three short years, before Kola, I and Timmy moved far away to Tasmania.

A year after you left us, your little grand-daughter, Tabitha passed away just a week before her second birthday on the 6th of February 1979.

After you died, Pop lived for another eighteen years, but the love and light of his life was gone. He grieved for you and then one day, after a lifetime of suppressing his original grief, he broke down and cried for his first wife and his three children. His grief was now fivefold, deep, and painful. Pop passed away 21st of February 1996, aged 81.

Three and a half years later, Kola passed away after a battle with cancer on the 15th of September 1999, aged 54.

I remember when you kept introducing those Ukrainian girls to Kola before we became engaged. I felt insecure. Once we were engaged, you accepted me totally. Now, after writing your life story and knowing all that you endured, I think I would have done the same thing.

I remember one day, standing at the bottom of the back steps of the house in Brisbane Street. You were standing above me and suddenly exclaimed, 'Oh you've got some grey hairs', and promptly, without asking, plucked them out. I guess by then, I was your daughter-in-law, and you were being Mum. While at first, it was a shock, I realised it was a mother's action. When you died, your hair was still thick and wavy and brown with not a grey hair in sight. At fifty, your skin was also beautiful.

My father and stepmother did nothing for our engagement or wedding, but you stepped in, opened your home, and organised a wonderful engagement party for us. Thank you, you are a true mother with a big heart.

You loved giving gifts. I remember how generous and loving you were. However, I remember one day receiving a gift from you, I didn't want! You and Pop still grew lots of vegetables and we were so often happy recipients. This day however, I was pregnant and suffering quite badly from morning sickness. One thing I absolutely could not deal with was the smell of celery. Well guess what! You handed me the biggest bunch of it, and I smiled and thanked you for it, and did your trick, which you used in your first pregnancy of holding it in. So, I smiled, and I gagged, and wished you would go home quick, so I could get rid of that offending, overpowering smell. Well, baby and I survived that day, and now I also grow celery and give away bunches of it.

Every time, we met; you would tell me snippets of your story. Your story fascinated me, and each time, after you left, I would write the information into a book which I kept. Ludmila, it is from these small memories you shared, that your story evolved.

I wrote your story in first person, as though I was you. The writing of your story will always be a very special part of my life. Through writing it, I felt as though I got to know you so much more.

Shortly before you were hospitalised and died, you and I were together in your house, alone. The children were asleep and Mykola, Kola and Walter had gone to see your doctor. You had lost the ability to speak. You came over to me with your hands clasped in the stance of prayer and dropped to your knees. I got onto my knees, hugged you, then held your hands and prayed with you. We didn't get our miracle that day, but our bond deepened, and even now when I remember, I do so with tears in my eyes

I loved your Ukrainian food. I remember the parties you gave and all those wonderful, tasty offerings. Well, Ludmila, I learnt to make borsche, vereniki, perushki and cabbage rolls.

While writing your story, I discovered what happened at Courtaulds Rayon Factory, where you both worked. At the end of the production line, the molten rayon would drip onto a tray. As it did so and began to harden, it would form wonderful fluid shapes, like the shapes that a candle makes as it melts and then resets. It became so hard it was unbreakable.

While upgrading my teaching qualifications, my research paper was based on education for the disadvantaged. As part of this, I went hunting for craft resources which would be affordable for low-income students. I found a big warehouse called Reverse Garbage. It was a wonderful treasure trove of resources from hundreds of industries who donated their 'garbage'; fibres, materials, threads, plastics, cardboard, paper. You name it, they had it. Amongst all of this 'garbage' I found a big bin full of these hardened, wax-like, rayon sculptures. I selected two and used them as decorations. Eventually they made their way into my garden.

As I was writing about your time at Courtaulds, I remembered them and went searching for them. The first was visible, the second one was buried beneath overgrown plants. I took them inside, scrubbed them clean and they are now again in my home. So Ludmila, I have two very tangible pieces of memorabilia directly linked to your life. A very special possession.

Also while researching your story, I found this information about Ukrainian folk-music, 'The most striking characteristic of authentic Ukrainian folk-music is the wide use of minor modes or keys which incorporate the augmented 2nd interval, invoking intense sadness when used melodically.'

In 2013, I published and recorded twelve pieces of piano music. In one of those pieces, ' Tabitha's Song', I went into the key of D minor and used the augmented interval melodically where the song was speaking of Tabitha's death. The words at that point are,

'Time to say goodbye, to shed those tears

LUDMILA

But time is brief and soon will pass those years

Time will be when we will sing and dance and live eternally'

Studying music, I had been taught to never use that interval, but I knew it was right for this song. When I performed it, I had a father come to me and hug me, with tears running down his face. I had a mum, a single young woman and others also respond with tears. The music struck a chord and unleashed deep emotions in these people.

Unknowingly, I had portrayed the death of my daughter by using this identifying mark of Ukrainian folk music. Not until nine years later, while writing your story did I discover what I had done, and the amazing link which I had formed.

My desire to be able to still see you and talk to you is like a two sided coin. On the one side, my wish is to have you here now, but on the other side of the coin, I am so glad you are not alive now, and protected from seeing what is happening in 2022 to your beloved people and your homeland.

Ludmila, you were part of the diaspora of Ukrainians having to flee their homeland to other countries around the world after the world war of 1939-1945. Now there is a new wave of refugees seeking refuge in other countries.

My hope is that your story can help those who are now in the position that you were in during the 1920s-1940s.

I love you. Your strength, resilience, courage and your beauty was such an inspiration. Your name, Ludmila, meaning 'Love for the people' shone out in your life.

Thank you for being my beautiful, caring mother-in-law, Marion.

AUTHOR'S NOTES

Ludmila shared memories of her life with me in the early 70s. I recorded these into an exercise book which I kept over the years. This became her story. It was a labour of love.

I had completed Ludmila's story, up to her arrival in Australia and Bonegilla Migrant Camp in 1949. I had written of the hard times under Stalin in her homeland, Ukraine, and under Hitler in the forced labour camp in Germany. I had just begun writing of her new life and being able to dream, be happy, be free and plan a new future in Australia, when in February 2022, life in Ukraine was once more thrown into turmoil when Putin and his Russian forces invaded Ukraine.

I struggled to write of the happy years at Bonegilla, while the TV was filled with the horrors taking place in that beautiful country and to those gentle people. At the same time, I felt it was imperative that I complete Ludmila's story and get it out there, in the hope that her story will bring hope to broken people, struggling with deep grief and loss as they try to pick up the torn threads of their lives and move forward into their future.

The first four sections of this story are written in Ludmila's voice. It is her story. When I had written her story, I added a letter to Ludmila from me, her daughter-in-law. It is a testament to her courage, her resilience and her determination to face life with a cup half-full.

BOOKS QUOTED OR CONSULTED

Applebaum Anne, Red Famine Stalin's War on Ukraine, Penguin Random House U K, 2017

Blanchard Tania, The Girl from Munich, Simon and Schuster (Australia) Pty Ltd,2017

Dale Helen, The Hand That Signed the Paper, Ligature Pty Ltd, 2017

Jaku Eddie, The Happiest Man on Earth, Pan Macmillan Australia Pty Ltd, 2020

Morris Heather, The Tattooist of Auschwitz, Echo Publishing, 2018

Parish Thomas, Encyclopedia of World War II, Simon and Schuster (Australia) Pty Ltd, 1978

Pennay Bruce, Sharing Bonegilla Stories, Albury Library Museum, 2012

Pennay Bruce, Albury Wodonga's Bonegilla, Albury Library Museum, 2001

Pennay Bruce, Picturing and Re-Picturing Bonegilla, Wodonga City Council, 2016

Articles, Contributions, Web articles, Newspapers

Wikipedia 1955 Hunter Valley Floods

The Great Flood of 1955

Forced Labour under German Rule during World War II

Osterbeiter

Certificate of Naturalization Ludmila Kiltschewskyj 1958

Christening Certificate Nicholaus (Mykola) Kiltschewskyj Wilhemsdorf 1945

Resettlement Registration Form- Ludmila Kiltschewskyj 1949

Resettlement Registration Form- Mykola Kiltschewskyj 1949

Resettlement Registration Form- Mykola Kiltschewskyj (son)1949

I.R.O. Resettlement Medical Examination Form Mykola Kiltschewskyj

I.R.O. Resettlement Medical Examination Form Ludmila Kiltschewskyj

I.R.O. Resettlement Medical Examination Form Mykola Kiltschewskyj (son)

ABOUT THE AUTHOR

Marion Kilchester was born in Hurstville, Sydney. She grew up on a small farm near Tamworth, New South Wales. Marion became a piano teacher, examiner, and a class-room music teacher. She has composed and published two books of music (arrangements/originals) which are listed in the Australian Guild of Music- Light Classical Recital Syllabus. She recorded a CD of these pieces. Marion also has a Diploma of Counselling.

Ludmila, is Marion's second book. Her first book, Though the Storms Rage Yet Will I Dance, is autobiographical/ counselling.

Marion at 77 is retired, enjoying her garden, her little dog, Hope, her home, her family, and friends. She is still composing and writing.

OTHER WORKS BY THE AUTHOR

- Though the Storms Rage Yet Will I Dance is an autobiography, telling how I learnt to dance through the many storms of my life such as the deaths of my mother, daughter and husband, attempted suicide, a childhood with an abusive stepmother and a father who could not or would not protect his children, and so much more. It is not a 'woe is me' story but a story of resilience and victory. At the end of each chapter are questions for self or group reflection.

- Reflections I - Printed music for piano, Grades 4-7, (7 pieces)

- Reflections II - Printed music for piano, grades 5-8, (5 pieces)

- Reflections CD - 12 Pieces for Piano

ACKNOWLEDGEMENTS

I would like to thank Margie and Walter Kiltschewskij for your willingness to answer all my questions and provide me with so much information, documents, and photos, without which this book would not be what it is. Thank you for your huge encouragement as I worked through Ludmila's story. You helped so much to bring your mother's story to life.

Thank you, Tim, for doing the cover for this book. Ludmila is your grandmother, Babushka, so there is no one more fitting to do this. She would be so proud of you.

Rick Aitchison, you got me through my first book, and again you helped me with the technology whenever I got stuck, which was often. Your extraordinary patience, your skill, and your willingness to come over every time I got stuck in a technological glitch, enabled me to complete the task. Thank you.

A huge thank you to Jo Wanmer and Jenny Tompkins for proofreading this book. I value your input greatly.

A big thank you to Majella Gee for designing my webpage and author page, the posters, and bookmarks, for answering my many calls, for so much. I could not have gotten here without you.

Big thank you to Jo Wanmer, Linda Upton, and Robert Brooke for reading and endorsing my book.

Thank you, Patty Beecham for designing my banner and reel. You are a treasure.

Thank you to Linda Upton for being my M.C. and for organising Events advertising. Nothing is too much or too hard for you.

Thank you to Beerwah Writers Group for your love and support. You are the best.

Thank you to the team at Disruptive Publishing. Thank you, Deborah Fay, Niva, and Joseph for turning this into a book I can be proud of and which honours Ludmila.

Many thanks to my family and many friends for always being there to support and encourage me.

www.ingramcontent.com/pod-product-compliance
Lightning Source LLC
Chambersburg PA
CBHW061735070526
44585CB00024B/2676